# TO BE THAT LIGHT

AN EXPERIENTIAL GUIDE TO SENIOR SEMINAR

William Hayashi

Lynne Copp

Marie Gillespie

Keri Kurlinski-Walters

Margie Nicholson

COLUMBIA

KENDALL/HUNT PUBLISHING COMPANY
4050 Westmark Drive     Dubuque, Iowa 52002

*Handwritten inscriptions:*

Dearest Carol –
Thank you for supporting us in designing our dreams, and may we support you in manifesting yours.
Great love and respect,
Bill

Carol, Gracias! Pa'lante, Pa'lante, Pa'lante para atrás ni para coger impulso! Cariño, Jisselle

Carol, thank you so much!

Carol,
Thank you my sister, Your Heart has captured my spirit, Together we shall Soar.
Love Valerie

Carol, your vision, enthusiasm, insight and patience are inspiring. Thank you for your grace and your guidance.
With great appreciation,
Margie

Carol, you're the model of what I want to be. Thank you so much for being a great coach.
Mary

CAROL, THANK YOU !! !!

TRUTH, BEAUTY, PEACE & LOVE —
ALL ELEMENTS THAT YOU HAVE BROUGHT, & FACILITATED INTO MY LIFE.
JOHN

Carol, May all your days be filled with joy. Love,
P.S. You bring the joy of "understanding" to so many.

Carol, Thank you for all that you have done. Thank you for investing in us and our students. I feel blessed to walk this spiritual path with you.
Love, Pate

Carol, the Johnny Appleseed of Senior Seminar – I am truly engaged in your leadership. Maggie

EXPERIENTIAL GUIDE TO SENIOR SEMINAR

# TO BE THAT LIGHT

Columbia College Mission Statement: Columbia is an undergraduate and graduate college whose principal commitment is to provide a comprehensive educational opportunity in the arts, communications, and public information, within a context of enlightened liberal education. Columbia's intent is to educate students who will communicate creatively and shape the public's perceptions of issues and events and who will author the culture of their times.

Layout and Design: Pamela Paulsrud

Copyright © 2002 by William Hayashi, Marie Gillespie and Margie Nicholson

ISBN 0-7872-9588-4

Printed in the United States of America
10 9 8 7 6 5 4 3 2 1

# ACKNOWLEDGMENTS

The teaching of Senior Seminar has been a collaborative endeavor from the beginning. This textbook would not have been possible without the deep dedication and skill of the many teachers who have taught Senior Seminar over the years. The materials within this textbook reflect a community willing to set their individual preferences aside for the benefit of students and the learning process. This community is also blessed with the undying support of our manager, Mary Harris. Any omissions of names are unintentional.

Brenda Anderson, Sherry Antonini, Stephen Asma, George Bailey, Doreen Bartoni, Nina Beaty, Bridget Boland, Doug Bonner, Patricia Buckley, Jotham Burrello, Julie Caffey, Barbara Calabrese, Paul Camic, Ed Childs, Paul Chirona, Barrie Cole, Pate Conaway, Kristen Cone, Lynne Copp, Laurie Cozad, Heather Davis, Joan Dickinson, Rose Economou, Valerie Ewing, Joy Foster, Sean Francis, Stephen Frech, Aaron Froelich, Fred Gardalphe, Josephina Gasca, Susan George, Johnny Gillespie, Marie Gillespie, Virginia Gordon, Jeffrey Gore, Myrna Hammerman, Gail Haus, Bill Hayashi, Lott Hill, John Huy, Sis Kiel, Caroline Kiesel, Ashley Knight, Keri Kurlinski-Walters, Kris Larsen, Sara Livingston, Pattie Mackenzie, Dirk Matthews, Jean McDonnell, Maggie McKenna, Mary Meadors, Joe Meno, Giselle Mercier, Suzanne Meyers, Paula Moscinski, Margie Nicholson, Paula Norbert, Sue Parcell, Pamela Paulsrud, Dia Penning, Andrea Peterson, Danuta Rojewska-Jirik, Solome Skaff, Theresa Sofianos, Nancy Soro, Doug Stapleton, Megan Stielstra, Susan Strong-Dowd, Elizabeth Sullivan, Lauren Targ, Wayne Teasdale, Jamie Thome, Sharon Warner, Rich Westley.

# CONTENTS

Columbia's **intent** is to educate students
who will **communicate creatively**
and **shape the public's perceptions** of issues and events
and who will **author the culture of their times.**

FROM THE COLUMBIA COLLEGE MISSION STATEMENT

*I only wanted to live in accord with the prompting which came from my true self. Why was that so very difficult?*

HERMAN HESSE

*To be nobody-but-yourself in a world which is doing its best, night and day, to make you every-body-else means to fight the hardest battle which any human can fight, and never stop fighting.*

e. e. cummings

In his introductory epigram to his novel *Demian*, the story of one youth's search to find his core self, the German novelist Herman Hesse ponders why this seemingly natural endeavor is so challenging. The American poet e. e. cummings responds that the struggle to be yourself is "the hardest battle which any human can fight, and never stop fighting." Why might this be so?

Just a few of the forces fighting against our coming into true personhood might be: parental expectations, media images, peer group pressure, internal scripting, and self-defeating inner programming. What are the consequences of living a life dictated by outer expectations and images rather than living from inside, from our own inner core of being and doing? Parents who feel that they've never pursued their dreams; peers who keep asking, "Is this all there is?"; "successful" adults going through midlife crises, seeking new partners and careers in hopes of finding themselves before dying—these are some of the results of living a programmed, inauthentic life. The salient question here is: Who am I, really? Hundreds of years ago, the Greek philosopher Socrates said: "The unexamined life is not worth living." Perhaps it is not so much a life "not worth living" as it is one empty of joy, meaning, and purpose, a life that finds its summation in temporary release and fleeting pleasures, a life based on the weekly exhortation, "Thank God it's Friday!"

As graduating seniors, you will be making many crucial decisions in the next months relating to work, relationships, where to live, prioritizing values, and so forth. These decisions and commitments will definitely affect how your future unfolds and the quality of your day-to-day existence. Senior Seminar, through exploring Voice, Values, and Vision, invites you to take some time before graduating to really contemplate, evaluate, and contextualize some of these decisions, asking you to consider where they come from and welcoming you to make them as much as possible from your own depth core and authentic personhood. To support this process of self-inquiry and values clarification, we've divided the course and this text into four chapters: contemplating self, serving community, designing vocation, and manifesting vision. Hopefully, these four themes will overlap and mutually support one another in guiding you to a clearer understanding of who you are and what you truly want from life. We take as our reference point this quotation from Shakespeare's *Hamlet*:

> This above all: to thine own self be true,
> And it must follow, as the night the day,
> Thou canst not then be false to any man.

We begin with the chapter on contemplating self. As the comedian Lily Tomlin said, "I always wanted to be somebody. I realize now that I should have been more specific." The clearer we are and the more fully we can stand behind our chosen identities, the more power we will have to manifest what we wish, and the happier and more fulfilled we will feel. The task of self-definition, however, is not always so easy nor so clear-cut. Oftentimes it is a process that evolves over time, requiring honesty, courage, and steady effort. Moreover, we are the only ones who can ever say with any certainty who we are and what we stand for. Many of the readings, exercises, discussion topics, and journaling contemplations in this unit invite you to observe your own inner life and consider the life choices you've already made as aids to identify what you most value and who you wish to become. As Thomas Jefferson so succinctly puts it, "If you don't know who you are, no one else will."

This process of self-definition is greatly reinforced by the support of like-minded individuals also working to know themselves. The Senior Seminar classroom ideally becomes a learning community where people feel safe to explore and share their stories, mutually respecting and honoring one another's self-discoveries and self-becoming. As we learn principles of community building and group trust within the classroom, we will be internalizing invaluable principles of team building and role definition that will serve us well in future work contexts of organizational planning and team support as well as preparing us for our role as engaged and responsible citizenry.

In contemplating self, we will explore three main areas: values, skills/gifts, and passions. When it comes time to choose a job, it will be helpful to know whether creative expression or financial security or friendly work environment matter most to us. Clarity and prioritizing of values can help us balance not only our career choices but also the whole larger arena of life meaning. Does staying with a community of supportive friends matter more than relocating to take the best entry-level position available in our field? How do we balance work, family life, spiritual growth, creative expression, physical well-being, intellectual enrichment, all, some, or more of these? In addition, we need to consider what our unique skills and gifts are. What comes naturally to us and what do we love to do yet need to work at? Do we go with what everyone tells us we should do because it's easy for us, or do we stay with what our heart tells us is our life path? This brings us to the question of life passions.

What activities, pursuits, relationships most inspire and enliven us? The great American choreographer and dancer Agnes de Mille writes this to her student and friend, Martha Graham: "There is a vitality, a life force, a quickening that is translated through you into action, and because there is only one of you in all time, this expression is unique. If you block it, it will never exist through any other medium. It will be lost. This world will not have it.

It is not our business to determine how good it is, how valuable it is, nor how it compares with other expressions. It is your business to keep it yours clearly and directly and to keep the channel open."

How do we identify such a life passion? What happens if we haven't yet discovered our path with heart? How do we keep our dream alive when there are no entry-level positions to support it? How do we balance living that dream and paying the bills? The first step in all of this is to see whether or not there is a spark, a seed, a blazing bonfire or a contained ember of passion, enthusiasm to guide and inform us. The Columbia College motto that inspired the title of this text is: "To be that light that I have seen." Where have you seen and experienced the light of inspiration, joy, fulfillment? What activities, interests have made you feel most alive and most yourself? Identifying and honoring this light of personal meaning and expression is the first and most fundamental step in the process of becoming. Without this light, life becomes a matter of paying the mortgage, living for the weekend or the three weeks of "paid" vacation, making sure the kids, at least, are taken care of. With this light, life becomes illumined, purposeful, and joyful. And as the scholar and mythologist Joseph Campbell says, "Follow your bliss and unseen hands will appear to open doors and show the way." At the very least, life will be an intense and ever-unfolding adventure.

The second chapter of the course, "Serving Community," reminds us that our journey to selfhood must include others—that, as Aristotle tells us, human beings are essentially "social" beings. What is meant by the "law of giving and receiving"? Why does the novelist E. M. Forster exhort, "Only connect"? As recent events in American history have all too clearly shown, without understanding, acceptance, mutual respect, and service, our very existence becomes threatened. The goals of "inter-being" and "global community" are no longer promising ideals but necessities of survival. In the months following September 11, 2001, the service professions and volunteer organizations experienced uncommon expansion and growth. Why, when our values and foundations have been shaken to their very roots, do we turn to civic engagement and human service to support and uplift us? Why does the experience of serving from our hearts sustain us even in our darkest hours?

We will begin the chapter on serving community by examining the communities that have supported, defined, and nourished us. How connected to and engaged are we with these communities now? What communities do we see ourselves belonging to and sustaining us in the future? What is the role of the artist within society; how consciously and in what contexts should artists consider their responsibilities to their audiences and the communities they influence? How do we find a balance between authentic and free self-expression and authoring the culture of our times in responsible and positive ways?

What exactly is the experience of service? Mother Teresa has said that "service is for joy." How do we move beyond seeing service as duty or externally imposed acts of "charity"? How do we taste the "nectar of service" that so many humanitarians and saints of all traditions have extolled? We will, perhaps, begin with "random acts of kindness" as individuals or a class and then move on to personal acts of service to people we know, listening to a friend, helping out a family member, supporting someone at work. The focus will be on the inner experience. What happens to the heart when we truly serve? In what sense is service a reciprocal act? In what ways do we receive as much as we give? How are "helping" and "fixing" different from "serving," and how do we come to recognize these differences internally?

We will move from individual service offerings to group or even whole class service projects. Researching, selecting, planning, offering, and reflecting on these group projects will help us internalize many valuable skills. How do we identify causes and concerns and decide collectively which ones to focus on? What values will help us prioritize our choices? How do we then organize and follow through as a group, a team? What roles do we play within the group, and how can we offer our special gifts, both organizational and creative, to a larger community?

What does it mean to interact with another community? How do we learn to empathize, watch, and listen for what that community needs rather than imposing our values, our projections, upon them? Finally, how do we reflect on the lessons and effectiveness of our undertaking? What have we learned, how have we been touched, and what role do we want service to play in our future lives?

In the first chapter, "Contemplating Self," the focus was primarily inward, on who we are and what we value. In this Chapter, the focus turns outward, on recognizing the needs of others and supporting them in ways that extend and nourish ourselves as well. We come to see how our values and passions and gifts become empowered, enhanced, enlarged through being shared, honed, and appreciated by others. We realize that it is in giving of what is most alive and vital within us that we become truly empowered, truly human. Ultimately we come to see that in serving others we are, in effect, only serving ourselves. As Norman Cousins has stated: "You will derive your supreme satisfaction not from your ability to amass things or to achieve superficial power but from your ability to identify yourselves with others and to share fully in their needs and hopes. In short, for fulfillment, we look to identification rather than acquisition."

Having contemplated our values, gifts, and passions, having experienced directly the power and meaning of service, we will now focus on our third Chapter, "Designing Vocation." Aristotle has said, "Where your talents and the needs of the world intersect, there lies your vocation." It is only when we bring our special gifts, values, and passions along with our understanding of service to our labor that work becomes vocation, career becomes calling. The great inventor and entrepreneur Henry Ford has said: "A business that makes nothing but money is a poor kind of business." The question of "right livelihood" has concerned conscious individuals of all generations, but only in our own day and times has the paradigm of work as both a "path with heart" and a "means of making a living" become so widespread and so accepted. Our parents, for the most part, did not conceive of work as self-expression nor joyful service. We now have both the opportunity and burden of choice.

This chapter on designing vocation is both practical and idealistic, pragmatic and inspirational. It begins with a questionnaire to help you determine how prepared you are in your own job search. Because people will be in so many different places in preparedness, interests, and motivation, this chapter more than any other can be used as an individual workbook with information and exercises to do or not do as you see fit. Topics include changes in the current work environment, deciding what you want and don't want from work, the art of networking, job search strategies, resume writing, informational and job interviewing, and much, much more. You will see how your previous contemplation of self, values, and passion affect your career choice and job search, how concerns of character and purpose and interest can enter your resumes, cover letters, and interviews, how service experience and interest in service can make you more marketable and actually affects your choice of a work environment and collegial atmosphere. We recommend that you read through all the material in the chapter and decide how much time and effort you want to expend in exploring, utilizing, and manifesting each section. There is much valuable information here, and only you can decide how best to use it. The opportunity exists to combine the profound and the practical, the humane and the pragmatic. Through exploring how best you can earn a living, you will discover much about who you truly and most deeply are. Joseph Campbell writes: "The decision as to what your career is to be is a very deep and important one, and it has to do with something like a spiritual requirement and commitment." The Sufi poet Rumi adds: "Everyone has been made for some particular work and the desire for that work has been put in his [or her] heart." This chapter will combine concerns of spirit and heart with the concrete particulars of how to research, seek out, and obtain meaningful work.

Our final chapter, "Manifesting Vision," like all the themes explored, focuses on the question of our individual and collective greatness. The mission statement of Senior Seminar reads: "To create learning communities within the classroom where people feel safe to explore and to become their greatness. Through exploring the four themes of contemplating self, offering service, designing vocation, and manifesting vision, we will realize who we are and all that we can become." The courageous author Marianne Williamson says, "We were born to make manifest the glory of God that is within us. It's not just in some of us, it's in everyone." And our own Senior Seminar graduate Ethel Nelson writes: "We each have something unique to offer the world; and it is up to us to find it and use it so that others can benefit from it."

To discover our greatness and offer it to the world for the upliftment of humanity requires the capacity to envision and to also implement what we see. It calls on that most free and most sacred of human faculties, the moral and creative imagination. As the American transcendentalist Henry David Thoreau puts it: "If you have built castles in the air, your work need not be lost; that is where they should be. Now put the foundations under them." So we have our imaginations, our capacity to dream, and our power to manifest or actualize those dreams.

To do this effectively, however, requires courage, commitment, and the letting go of limiting beliefs and irrational yet long-held self-concepts. As the contemporary film *Waking Life* asks: "What keeps us from actualizing our full potential, becoming our greatness? One of two things—fear or laziness." We need to look at and identify those aspects of ourselves that fear and undermine our greatness. We need to look at those old tapes that keep us restricted and inauthentic. Fortunately we will have had the support and experience of the three previous chapters. We will have already contemplated who we are, what we value, and what we most long to give to others. We will have learned to recognize the promptings of the heart, the language of spirit, and the disciplined focus of our intellects and wills. We will have understood our passions, our gifts, and why sharing them with others makes them sing. We will have developed eyes that see and honor our own greatness and that of every other member of our classroom community. It is up to us to now consider how our life work, our chosen vocation or calling, can be a living expression of what is most alive and sacred within us. It is now up to us to name and make real our dreams, to hold and polish them so they can take on living flesh.

To help us do this we will create a personal mission statement that will name the attributes of a personally meaningful and significant life for each one of us as well as identify some different roles we would like to play in the future to live balanced and whole lives. We will then create a plan of action, identifying some clear action steps we can take now and in subsequent stages to begin realizing our vision. We will articulate goals and explore resources, both inner and outer, to actualize our intentions. Finally, we will have specific and concrete practice in manifesting our visions through the creation and sharing of our final vision project, a creative expression in the medium of our choice of who we are, offering the best and brightest of ourselves to impact and transform the communities and audiences we most wish to serve and uplift.

This is a lot to accomplish in a single semester. Yet individual students and entire Senior Seminar communities have done it in the past. We can take the inspiration of the German poet and philosopher Goethe, who writes: "Whatever you can do, or dream you can, begin it. Boldness has genius, power, and magic in it." What we need is clear intention, absolute faith in ourselves, and the unconditional support of a community of fellow seekers willing to recognize and celebrate that greatness in others that they see and honor in themselves. As the great meditation master Swami Muktananda has said: "Honor yourself, love yourself, respect yourself, worship yourself, because God dwells within you as you." A challenging task? As the Greek pragmatist Aristotle has commented: "Noble things are difficult."

May you experience the blessings of your own greatness.

Bill Hayashi
Director, Senior Seminar

# chapter 1

**CONTEMPLATING SELF**

| | objective | outcome | readings | other elements |
|---|---|---|---|---|
| **unit 1** | Create a learning community that supports authentic self-reflection and group cohesion. | Students can respectfully listen to one another's sharing of their inner lives, supporting each other's growth. Students participate freely and with authenticity in group discussions and activities. | *Community* *Honoring Greatness* *Blue Lou's Gift* | Name Game Community Building Partner Interviews Establishing Learning Community Guidelines Class Rituals Discerning Excellence Special Quality Contemplation |
| **unit 2** | Incorporate self-reflection on a regular basis. | Students contemplate self through writing in their journals both in class and at home, through classroom activities and reflective papers. | Daily Journaling and Passions *On Keeping a Notebook* | Visual Self-Reflection Journaling Patterns Giving and Receiving Feedback What, So What, Now What? |
| **unit 3** | Identify and prioritize core values. | By reviewing their past through activities, guided contemplations, and a reflective paper, students clarify core values and future intentions guided by these values. | Student Samples | Treasured Object Your Definition of Success Values Visualization Values Inquiry Values and People Values Budget |
| **unit 4** | Identify personal passions and what role those passions may play in the future. | Through classroom activities and projects, students can identify, celebrate, and express those passions that make them feel most alive and in the experience of flow. | Flow *Flow* Your Heart Song *Listening for the Deeper Music* Prose, Poetry, and Passion *The Teachings of Don Juan* *The Last Hours* *The Journey* *Poetry* Passion Paper Samples | Personal Flow Questionnaire Music that Resonates Describing Your Heart Song Passion Mapping Passion Paper Passion Paper Workshop |

## CONTEMPLATING SELF

*If you don't know who you are, no one else will.*

THOMAS JEFFERSON

*What lies behind us and what lies before us are tiny matters, compared to what lies within us.*

RALPH WALDO EMERSON

The words and images imbedded in the culture of humankind frequently relay the importance of contemplating self. We relentlessly seek out or haphazardly stumble upon aphorisms and nod our heads, forward them to others, or expound upon them over a cup of espresso. We, by chance, see ourselves and laugh or cry or look the other way. We rely on the tremulous arts to lead the way and inspire us to question ourselves and our planetmates. It's a bit easier when things are disguised as arts to embrace what we like and critique and spit out what grabs us by the throat. We drift along affably savoring what pleasures we eke, until something tiny or gargantuan happens to shatter terra firma. And then the questions roll as heavily as thunder in a midnight stormy sky.

**who**
am I?
What's
**important**
to me?
What do I
**love** to do and **be?**
**Why**
Where am I here?
am I going?

When the questions roll forth, it is helpful to have a way for seeking answers. There are as many paths as there are people on this planet. What sends one to the waterfront may send another to the mountaintop and another to a party and another to a religious retreat and another into the arms of a loved one. What starts one writing may start another dancing and another singing and another painting and another composing verse and another sailing and another boxing and another cooking. We find answers in another's eyes and in the sunrise and in the laugh of a child and the smell of a flower. We find answers that carry us along until the next something comes along to shatter that upon which we think we stand. We question, we seek, we draft answers, and do it over and over until we realize that what we honor in this process is the universal experience of growth.

And we become.

The art of contemplating self is about looking within and discovering the seeds of our greatness. How do we look within? By trying things out. Never written in a journal? Give it a try. Never sketched? Give it a try. Never sat on a beach silently watching the surf and sky? Give it a try. You may discover more about your patterns of self-contemplation than your mind has allowed. Experience it all. Then choose. And choose again.

The art of contemplating self is also about embracing it as an ongoing part of your life. Every day is an opportunity to grow or to be swept away with the surf of a hurried society. You choose. When you find a way to embrace self-reflection on a daily basis, it will be as refreshing as breathing freely. You will restore your mind, body, and soul.

As you dive into this chapter, you'll continue your journey of contemplating self. Together we will explore community, reflection, values, and passion. We will discover how contemplating ourselves is the beginning of understanding and embracing our greatness.

*Our deepest fear is not that we are inadequate. Our deepest fear is that we are powerful beyond measure....Your playing small doesn't serve the world.*

MARIANNE WILLIAMSON

*Don't be afraid your life will end; be afraid that it will never begin.*

GRACE HANSEN

self within

# community

## unit one

**COMMUNITY**

**NAME GAME**

**COMMUNITY BUILDING**

**PARTNER INTERVIEWS**

**ESTABLISHING LEARNING COMMUNITY GUIDELINES**

**CLASS RITUALS**

**HONORING GREATNESS**

**BLUE LOU'S GIFT**

**DISCERNING EXCELLENCE**

**SPECIAL QUALITY CONTEMPLATION**

*Objective: Create a learning community that supports authentic self-reflection and group cohesion.*

## SELF WITHIN COMMUNITY

*Objective: Create a learning community that supports authentic self-reflection and group cohesion.*

*The single most common finding from a half-century's research on the correlates of life satisfaction, not only in the United States but around the world, is that happiness is best predicted by the breadth and depth of one's social connections.*

ROBERT PUTNAM

When we meet together on the first day of class, we have the potential to become a brand new community... a learning community. We all have something to offer the group, and together we can support each other as we grow. We will establish a learning community that supports authentic self-reflection, sharing of talents and gifts, and group cohesion. Our learning community will help us embrace our greatness and become all that we can be.

However, just being together in the same place on the same day at the same time does not mean we have community. So what is it that makes a community work? And how can we make this community a vibrant arena for learning? We will explore these questions and develop our skills so that we may respectively listen to one another's sharing of our inner lives and support each other's growth. We will create an atmosphere in which we can participate freely and with authenticity in discussions, activities, and just being.

## COMMUNITY

by Joe Meno

High school, 1988. As a kid in a punk band, we did not know how to play our instruments. We did not know how to write good songs. Worse, we did not have anything to sing about, not that we were aware of anyway. We were too young, too dumb, too insignificant to have anything to say. Our singer, Brian, would sing so fast so no one would know that his lyrics were complete nonsense. If someone did stop by the garage where we practiced, a friend, someone's girlfriend, she would stand there and nod and then walk away confused, wondering what they had just seen and heard.

And yet, the other guys in the band and I were part of something, something most definitely bigger than us, our small worlds and worries, we were part of a group of kids who hung out at the mall or by the Tastee-Freeze with greasy hair and leather jackets and safety-pins run through holes in our jeans. We defined ourselves by the way we looked and so you could identify a punk by his blue liberty Mohawk or black combat boots walking down along the other side of the street. We were never alone, and even so, in our bedrooms, at our jobs, there were always the music, which was the center of it all, the bands, the songs that we all knew and would sing loud driving around in someone's older brother's car. What drove the punk scene, after all, wasn't hair dye and goofy haircuts and torn concert tee-shirts, it was the music. Behind the music was the various bands' general notion that everyone, everywhere in the world, was created equal and had an equal right to respect, hope, and dignity.

•

As a writer and artist now, I believe it is my responsibility to serve my audience, my readers, in helping them see the connection between their lives and the lives of the rest of the world around them. Technology and time have made it more difficult to feel any sort of connection with the daily strangers we pass on the street, our neighbors, our coworkers, and yet, within us, is a fierce need for human connection, a need so fierce we find ourselves seeking it out in strange ways; through television, movies, novels, we find the companionship and human warmth so many of us are missing. Throughout the semester, we see the need and importance of community: how it influences our values, how it supports our voices, how it helps define our creative passion, the need for community involvement and service, and finally, how we as artists must use our joy, our powers, to serve the needs of the world, in order to continue to grow as communicators and humans, through in-class discussions, community-building exercises, and our willingness to be honest with who we truly are.

●

## Controversial Questions. One immediate way

community challenges and inspires us to grow both as artists and as people is through direct interaction with the wisdom of fellow human beings. Not simply the "Hello there," or "How was your day?" conversations but through actual human dialogue where we are able to move to a kind of understanding beyond our own perspectives. Though we all have a deeply felt need to understand and be understood, sometimes, because of the pace of modern life, we are unable to engage in these kinds of thoughtful, personal conversations. The strength of the seminar lies in the wisdom of the individual students, their voices, their visions, their passions, and in the class' ability, as a functioning community, to listen, not just respond, but to allow ourselves to be moved, transformed, changed, by what some other human has to offer. This, again, is the most basic action of any worthwhile art.

A way to help foster these kinds of productive, life-changing conversations is through in-class discussions that respond to various questions that ask us to make decisions on what and why we value what we do. These "controversial questions," or questions that force us in some way to make a judgment of value, not only allow us to develop a degree of self-awareness of who we have come to be, but also allow us, as a community, to listen to the deeper wisdom of our fellow human beings. Some examples of controversial questions follow, with clarifying statements and response questions, which may be used to help us find value in ourselves and our fellow classmates.

*Is family/community still necessary in our world? Does "family" still hold any purpose? What are the benefits of family/community? What are the evils? How are we, as individuals, defined, supported, and limited by our communities? How does art work to define community? How does art work to help us see the value in communities?*

*Is it possible to put a value on one piece of art over another? How? What are the criteria? Should everyone be allowed to express themselves? Is censorship ever necessary?*

**NAME GAME**

Community building begins with learning one another's names. Playing the "name game" combines learning names with having fun. One version is for each person to think of an adjective that starts with the same letter as their first name, e.g., Beneficent Bill. Beneficent Bill starts, and then the next person repeats his name and then shares their own name plus an adjective. The game continues until the last person shares not only their name and descriptor but that of every other person in the community. Other versions are to make up a rhyme and gesture for your name—Bill has will—while pounding one's fist. Again, the game is to keep adding more and more people and their names.

## COMMUNITY BUILDING

Beyond in-class discussions, there are a few very simple ways we develop a deeper understanding of the grace and wisdom of our fellow students. Most of us feel our art best represents who are, what we feel, and our vision of the world. By interacting through art, by allowing ourselves to take part in a collaborative artistic effort, we again open ourselves to experience new perspectives, new ideas, new ways of negotiating the world. Some examples of simple community-building activities follow:

•At the beginning of class, students take out a piece of paper, without writing their names at the top. Very quickly and as clearly as they can, students write down the "story" of their first kiss. After about five minutes of writing, the stories are collected and then re-distributed, so that each student now has a story to read. After reading the stories, some are selected to be read out loud. Very quickly it becomes obvious how story, and art itself, works to create connections between simple strangers, by dealing with the very human moments of our lives and seeing the joy, pain, and value in them. Discuss parallels between film, dance, photography in relaying your moments of being with others.

•Assemble the students in small groups or partners. Consider the needs of the world, such as "laughter," "joy," "wonder," "companionship," and then assign a need to each group. Give each group ten minutes to decide how, right now, they might use their skills as artists to meet this need; a visual art piece, a conceptual design, a performance work, maybe something as simple as opening doors and saying hello. Now give students the important opportunity to put these ideas into action. Give each group ten minutes to create and perform their work, outside of the class, and then discuss their responses. How did they affect the community? How did they meet the particular need of the world? Is one small deed more powerful than any grand intention?

How have America's values changed in the last fifty years? How has this affected you? Your art? Who creates the values behind art? Is the world better off now?

What does it mean to love, beyond yourself? Is all love self-serving? Is it possible to maintain love throughout time? What's the connection between the stories we hear above love and the reality? Can you be successful without love?

What is more important, process or product, when it comes to art?

Are some people destined to be great? How do genetics, class, free will play a part? How does knowing your passion play a role in manifesting your destiny? Does everyone really have a chance?

When have you been touched by fate or destiny?

Are you really responsible to the world around you? How? Who has the power in society? Who has the ability to change society? How?

In the future, what will you have, what will you be doing, owning, what will it take for you to be successful? Where does God or spirit come into play? What relevance does God/spirit have in the modern world?

Is evil part of human nature? Is evil a natural part of our world, ourselves? Why are we still wrestling with evil? Where does art work in fighting these forces?

What does it mean to be authentic? Is it necessary? How does it limit success? How does it help you get what you want? Are you authentic? Are you honest?

Is long-term happiness achievable? How? Are failure, grief, depression part of the human story? Is conflict part of our stories? Is happiness genetic? How does life purpose/mission play a role in our happiness?

What happens after death? How do we cope with change/transition? What stories prepare us for what lies in the great beyond, the next phase of our lives?

By asking these questions, and truly being open to our peers' responses, we not only invite a sense of community, shared learning, and true human understanding, we clarify our own values, our own sense of purpose, and our sense of self.

·

## Conclusion.
Art, finally, is about relationships: the artist's relationship between the audience, the relationships in our lives, mother and daughter, father and son, brother and sister, men and women, young and old, alive and dead, our true selves and the world raging around us. Art allows us to see the inner workings of these relationships, to realize and rethink their importance, so in turn, we are able help others find value and meaning in their own lives. Who we are, as humans, as artists, is the very complicated result of who our parents are, the neighborhood where we grew up, the music we listened to as a teenager, the movies we've seen, the TV shows we've watched, who we are in love with. Again and again, through our interactions with other human beings, we are changed, we are pushed to grow, we are led to a greater understanding of ourselves, of what we have to offer. Community, in the end, is the sum total of our individual personal reflections. As artists, then, we are always working to discover who we are and our responsibilities to the world around us.

## PARTNER INTERVIEWS

As we continue to grow together as a learning community, it is important that we get to know each other. With the Partner Interviews, we can begin the one-on-one bonding and deepen the community-building process. Following the interviews, each person is introduced to the entire learning community. As we introduce our partners, we can communicate to the group what stood out most about this person. When deciding on what to ask your partner, it is good to include both fun and in-depth questions. The instructor may have some suggestions as well.

Possible Questions to Ask Your Partner:

*What name would you like to be called in class?*

*What are you studying? Why?*

*What's your favorite type of music and/or recording group?*

*What do you like to do when you just want to have fun?*

*What do you spend the most time worrying about right now?*

*In what situation or activity do you feel most yourself, most empowered?*

*How would you describe this feeling?*

*What quality do you most like about yourself and why?*

*What do you see as your life purpose?*

*What were some of the main communities, groups, institutions that shaped and guided you as a child, as a teenager?  Which of these continue to play a part in your life?*

*What role did music and different musical groups play in influencing your values and lifestyle?*

*A Beatles song says, "I get by with a little help from my friends."  How true is this for you?  What are some other communities that influence, support, frustrate you at the present time?*

*What might be some other "controversial questions" that you would like to discuss with your classmates?*

*What might be some other "first time" stories you would want to explore?  Are there other "needs" you'd like to see brought into awareness through community art making?*

# ESTABLISHING LEARNING COMMUNITY GUIDELINES

As our experience of participating in a learning community grows, it is important to cocreate a list of principles to facilitate comfortable and authentic conversation. While we have taken some time to get to know one another and share some relaxing, fun experiences, it is very likely that we have already begun conversations about how important it is to have some community guidelines and values.

What are some examples of guidelines that other learning communities have established? One group included the following on their list: having a positive attitude, being open-minded, listening, providing supportive encouragement to each other, focusing on material that is thought-provoking and relevant, mutual respect, and participating in group experiences. Another group included these things on their guideline list: honoring and respecting diversity, valuing each member, listening, creating an interactive experience, observing one another, allowing chaos to lead to creation, handling confrontation through compromise, and providing encouragement to one another.

There are many ways to go about discussing and deciding upon community guidelines. One possibility is to look to past experiences. Recall a community you've belonged to that really worked (sports team, club, organization, or a particular family experience). Visualize the experience as concretely as possible. Write down in your journals the different qualities that allowed this experience to be so positive. What was it that supported this group becoming a cohesive unit?

With your learning community share aloud the harmonizing qualities you discovered about that former community experience. After reflecting as a group on these qualities that have been a part of other communities, we can generate together a list of guidelines we feel will help support the creation of this community as harmonious and supportive within the classroom. Copies of this list can be provided for everyone, or the list can be posted on the wall (large and easily readable) during each meeting.

A simpler alternative to this method would be to have each member of the learning community think about their response to the following question: What guidelines do you need to feel safe and open to share in a community setting? From individual responses to the question, we can work together to finalize our community list.

Once agreed upon, we can use these guidelines to monitor our conversations within the learning community. We can also gently remind one another when they are being ignored. Since we have created the guidelines through consensus, we will each feel more committed to them and to each other.

## CLASS RITUALS

We have established the guidelines we wish to follow for our learning community. However, we all lead busy and involved lives. As we enter the learning community for each class meeting, we have many things on our minds and in our hearts. As each class begins, it is important that we feel that we can take a moment to share those things briefly. If we have a sense of each other's physical, mental, and emotional state, we can support each other more fully as we interact as a group. It is also important within our learning community to stimulate genuine, engaged dialogue right from the beginning of class. Therefore, our community may want to agree upon some routines or rituals for beginning the class each time.

One ritual for beginning class is to have a check-in period. The check-in period could focus on members sharing their primary physical/emotional state. It could be a time to report on goals. It also could be a time to share with the group what has happened since the last meeting. Another option is to use this time to share announcements about upcoming events at school. Announcements can certainly include community members sharing information about upcoming events in which they are involved: show openings, performances, publications coming out, and more.

Another compelling way to begin class is to use a provocative quote and/or question and/or position statement related to the day's theme to generate authentic conversation. Community members can journal quietly and also discuss the questions/quote. All are encouraged to share what they really think and feel. It is not a matter of being right or wrong but rather of speaking your truth. The more authentic and spontaneous our responses, the more lively and engaging our conversation. It's a great way for us to find our voices and offer different points of view.

## HONORING GREATNESS

As we continue this journey as a learning community, we begin to get a glimpse of our own greatness and the greatness of the others. Based on an ancient myth, the following story can be the spark for us to contemplate the impact of looking for and honoring each other's greatness. The experience of exploring this text together will further strengthen our community bond. It will inspire us to really see the light within ourselves and reflect that greatness to the world.

# BLUE LOU'S GIFT

by Megan Stielstra

Slam Dango was something. I'm telling you, this band could rock. ROCK. You'd be walking down the street and see their posters slathered up on the wall—you know the ones I'm talking about: they had this basketball player slamming a great big skull through a hoop with the words *this could be your head* scrolled underneath—cool, huh?—so you'd go to whichever hole-in-the-wall indie rock club they were playing at that night. The place would be packed, let me tell you, these guys could fill a room with screaming kids all waving their fists in the air, pounding their heads up and down like they didn't have control of their limbs anymore, and you'd hear your own heart beating in your ears—louder, louder, louder—and know you were a part of something huge.

But like any indie rock band in Chicago, after a while Slam Dango started falling out. Maybe it was that lousy review that electronic zine had given their third album. Maybe it was Rambone's over on Fullerton getting shut down by the health department. There were all these new bands to compete with, too, these new-fangled multi-media groups that projected films on the wall while they rocked out, and what about everybody listening to hip hop all the time? Man, it sucked!

The guys stood around their practice space and talked about it one day. Like, is it the music? Do we need to change our direction or something? Is it us? Have we lost it? Should we quit while we're ahead?

"No way, man!" said Juice. He played the bass and could get really excited. "It's not us! It's, like, the Chicago scene! It's like everybody's just playing for other musicians, you know, not for the people!"

Delco on guitar agreed. "The people know, man," he said. "They know we rock."

"They used to know," said Monty behind his drums. "They KNEW, like, past-tense, man." He whacked his cymbals to punctuate his words. Ba-dum bum.

Gus sat quietly on his amp listening to all that was said. He'd been with the band since the beginning, through three albums and four bass players, endless nights in the back of the van doing bit shows in bit cities, crowd after crowd after crowd. He'd watched as that crowd grew from one or two people—their girlfriends, roommates, and sometimes their moms—to huge groups coming out and coming together around the music. And now the crowds were starting to shrink and he didn't know if he could handle watching it go the other way.

"I gotta clear my head," he said, and walked out of the room.

Down the street from their practice space was this little dive bar with really cheap beer. Gus ordered a High Life and turned to find a table. Off in the corner he saw Ol' Blue Lou, killing Wild Turkey and sitting by himself. That wasn't any surprise—any time you went there you'd see Blue Lou and his whiskey—he was an all-day, everyday sort of drunk. But Gus had heard that Lou'd played harmonica with the Ray Coolidge Trio, so last time he was in Backbeat Records he went to the blues section and looked for their album. There were like eight of them, and there on the back cover was Ol' Blue Lou, looking young, looking clean, a harp in his hands and a sparkle to his teeth. Louis Simmons was his name, and the album had all these blurbs about how great he was: *Louis Simmons does for the Blues what your Mama does for chicken soup! and In case you ain't got nothin' to cry over, Lou Simmons'll have you weeping in your whiskey! and It don't get Bluer than Blue Lou!* Gus took a long pull off his beer and started walking over to the Bluesman's table.

If anybody could tell him what was what, it'd be Louis Simmons.

"Mind if I sit down?" he asked the old man.

Blue Lou grinned. "You betcha, boy," he said, and he welcomed Gus to his table. But when Gus explained the purpose of his visit, the old Bluesman could only raise his glass, down his whiskey, and commiserate. "Don't gotta tell me twice, my friend," he said. "Same thing happened in my day. S'like the music has gone out of people." So the Bluesman and the Rock Star drank together, slamming back shots of Wild Turkey, telling stories that began with the words *back when,* and as the night wore on their voices got louder and their words were slurred. The bartender called last call and Gus staggered to his feet. He couldn't hold his liquor as well as Lou and he wobbled a little. "I was supposed to be back," he said. "I was supposed to be back like forever ago or something really long like that."

Lou laughed. "Was good to have met you, kid," he said, and held out his hand to the Rock Star.

Gus felt very drunk and very confused. He wanted simultaneously to be exactly like Ol' Blue Lou, and nothing at all like Ol' Blue Lou. He took the hand the Bluesman offered him and leaned forward. "I'm just worried," he whispered, looking left, looking right, looking for anyone who might overhear what he was about to admit, "that we've forgotten how to rock."

Lou shook his head. "Don't go thinking like that, kid," he said.

Gus felt very desperate all of a sudden. He grabbed the old man by the shoulders and shook him a little. "You gotta give me something man, I'm serious. There's gotta be something we can do!"

Ol' Blue Lou was calm and cool. "Sorry, Rock-and-Roll," he said. "I got no advice to give. The only thing I can tell you is that the rock is in one of you."

When Gus returned to the practice space, his fellow band mates crowded around him.

"Dude, you've been gone for, like, six hours."

"What is up with you, man?"

"Dude," Ba-dum bum. "Are you drunk?"

Gus sat down on the floor so he wouldn't fall. "I had a couple with Ol' Blue Lou," he said. Steady. Steady.

"The drunk guy?"

"No, man, he was a musician. Like, a good one."

"An amazing one."

"So what'd he say?"

"He didn't say anything," Gus answered. He found a guitar next to him and strummed it a little bit. "We just drank, and talked a bit about the music scene—"

"S'all crap, man!" Juice yelled. "It's like all the musicians are just playing for each other inst—"

"Chill out, man!"

"Yeah, dude. What were you saying, Gus?"

Gus had been asking himself the same question. "He did say this one thing that was kinda weird," he remembered.

"Yeah? What was that?"

"He said the rock was in one of us."

The guys all stopped talking and thought about that for a minute.

"The rock is in one of us?" one of them repeated, to make sure they'd heard correctly.

"The rock is in one of us," said Gus again.

So for the next few weeks, the guys all thought about what Lou said. The rock is in one of us? Was he talking about one of the guys in the band? If that's what was what, then which one? He must have meant Gus, right? Yeah, if he meant anyone, he probably meant Gus. He's the lead singer. He writes all the songs. But on the other hand, it was the guitar that made the music, right? And that'd be Delco, and you KNOW Delco rocked. I mean, when Eddie from Mustard Seed left Mustard Seed to start his own band he tried to come in and STEAL Delco, and Eddie from Mustard Seed knows, you know! And he couldn't have meant Juice 'cause that guy's, like, crazy! Like he's got this agenda or something and never wants to—but, wait, he's the one that gets us to work together, you know, as a GROUP. He's the one that's like, "Gus, shut up for a minute and listen to what Delco is playing there. What can you do with that?" and you know the low end is what holds all the music together anyhow, so maybe Juice really is the one that rocks. But, you know, Monty rocks, too, 'cause he's the one who reminds us that we're doing a good job, you know. He's the one who'll stop practice and be like, "Dude, this ROCKS!" Or, "Juice, that line that you just played there was awesome!" So maybe he meant Monty. He could've meant any of us! Except for me, I mean. He couldn't have meant me. That's just nuts, you know. There isn't anything special about me. But what if there is? What if the rock is in me?

As they wrote and practiced and hung out and thought about all this, the guys in the band treated each other better on the slim chance that one of them might have the rock. And on the even slimmer chance that each guy himself might have the rock, they began to treat themselves better. They listened to each other more, and talked about their ideas, and got comfortable taking risks. They practiced more on their own—trying out new things—so when they came together every week in their space it was like: "heeeey, check this out! And this! And this! And how can all these sounds work together as one big sound?"

And get this: other bands would be going to their own practice spaces, and they'd hear the music coming from underneath Slam Dango's door, and they'd stop to listen. And after practice, when they'd meet their girlfriends out at bars on the near Northside, they'd talk about the music they'd heard. So when the posters starting appearing around town for the next show, people showed up to hear the music. And they told more people and they told more people and they filled the clubs and drank cheap beer and stood there together with one big communal heartbeat that got louder and louder in their ears, and they pounded their heads up and down together, and they were all together.

And you know what else? Some of the younger kids in the crowd heard Slam Dango's music and started talking to each other. And they found out that he plays the bass and I play the drums and my brother plays bass so do you want to come over sometime this weekend and jam with us in the garage? Hell, yeah, man! It'll ROCK! So within a few years there were more bands, and more, and the next time you're in Backbeat Records you should check out some of them. Read the blurbs on the backs of their albums and maybe you'll see that Slam Dango was one of their major influences, you know, one of the bands that made them want to play music. All thanks to Blue Lou's gift.

*What is Blue Lou's gift?*

*What happens to the band Slam Dango and why?*

*What do you think is the author's message?*

*When have you experienced the impact of someone's recognizing your greatness?*

*What gets in the way of recognizing someone's good qualities, and what can you do about that?*

*How might we apply the message of the story to our classroom?*

## DISCERNING EXCELLENCE
## THROUGH SHARING ACHIEVEMENTS

One way that we may celebrate our special qualities with one another is through sharing of past experiences and projects that we feel show evidence of our greatness. This will also deepen our bond as a learning community.

We can also look at these projects and experiences and begin to explore what excellence means to us. Excellence is something we strive to achieve in our endeavors. We have standards for ourselves and we have external standards (employers, certification procedures, submission guidelines). Therefore, it is important to discern what constitutes excellence. We can then strive to achieve those standards on a regular and consistent basis.

We can bring in to class an example of something we created/achieved of which we feel particularly proud; something we believe is excellent. It could be a work of visual art, performing art, media art, writing, an award or honor representing an accomplishment, or other.

We can each share this achievement with the others by showing it and/or speaking about it. At the end of each presentation, we can write a brief note to the presenter about what stood out most about what they brought in to share. It is important that our comments focus entirely on positive elements at this time. It can also be nice to sign our name to the notes. These brief notes are given to the presenter.

When each person has had a chance to present, we can generate a list of three to five qualities we believe exist in our individual work and help to define it as excellent. We can write these thoughts in our journals or share them in discussion.

With this information, we can begin to discuss and generate together a list of five to seven qualities that everyone agrees are in general essential to excellent work. We can each strive to generate our class work guided by these standards of excellence. We can also look at other community members' work in search of evidence that the agreed-on qualities are present in the work.

*There is no greater agony than bearing an untold story inside you.*

MAYA ANGELOU

**SPECIAL QUALITY CONTEMPLATION**

Think of someone in your life to whom you are special. It could be a family member, friend, partner, pet, etc. What's one quality they value in you, that makes you special to them? We can then each tell the others in the learning community who that person is that sees us as special and name the quality that person values in us. It can be helpful for each member of the learning community to have a list of each person and their special quality.

As we remember the impact of seeing and honoring one another's greatness as expressed in the story we read, we can explore how we might remember to look for and acknowledge one another's greatness and special qualities. For it is truly within the process of sharing and acknowledging our greatness that we build a deep community bond.

# reflection

## unit two

*Objective: Incorporate self-reflection on a regular basis.*

**DAILY JOURNALING AND PASSIONS**

**ON KEEPING A NOTEBOOK**

**VISUAL SELF-REFLECTION**

**JOURNALING PATTERNS**

**GIVING AND RECEIVING FEEDBACK**

**WHAT, SO WHAT, NOW WHAT?**

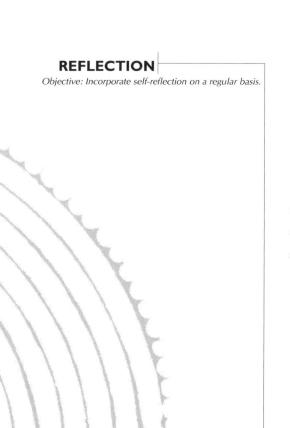

## REFLECTION

*Objective: Incorporate self-reflection on a regular basis.*

*There is a vitality, a life force, a quickening, that is translated through you into action, and because there is only one of you in all time, this expression is unique. If you block it, it will never exist through any other medium. It will be lost.*

AGNES DE MILLE

We have shared some experiences that have provided a growing sense of connection within our learning community. We will grow even closer through many more shared experiences during the semester.

These shared experiences have undoubtedly revealed things about ourselves. We have been able to contemplate and reflect on various issues while being immersed within the group experience. In Unit Two we will concentrate on looking deeply within ourselves using a variety of techniques. We will begin to explore those things that make us feel most alive. We will also begin to discover how we can make the most of giving and receiving feedback. Finally, we will take a look at a reflective process that we can share with our learning community which will allow us to reflect together on our group experiences.

## DAILY JOURNALING AND PASSIONS

## In the quiet moments of our day we can reflect on our lives.

Journaling is one method of self-reflection that can be very effective when used on a daily basis. Read the following article about the power of using journals.

excerpts from

# "On Keeping A Notebook"

So the point of my keeping a notebook has never been, nor is it now, to have an accurate factual record of what I have been doing or thinking. That would be a different impulse entirely, an instinct for reality which I sometimes envy but do not possess. At no point have I ever been able successfully to keep a diary; my approach to daily life ranges from the grossly negligent to the merely absent, and on those few occasions when I have tried dutifully to record a day's events, boredom has so overcome me that the results are mysterious at best. What is this business about "shopping, typing piece, dinner with E, depressed"? Shopping for what? Typing what piece? Who is E? Was this "E" depressed, or was I depressed? Who cares?

In fact I have abandoned altogether that kind of pointless entry; instead I tell what some would call lies. "That's simply not true," the members of my family frequently tell me when they come up against my memory of a shared event. "The party was not for you, the spider was *not* a black widow, *it wasn't that way at all.*" Very likely they are right, for not only have I always had trouble distinguishing between what happened and what merely might have happened, but I remain unconvinced that the distinction, for my purposes, matters. The cracked crab that I recall having for lunch the day my father came home from Detroit in 1945 must certainly be embroidery, worked into the day's pattern to lend verisimilitude; I was ten years old and would not now remember the cracked crab. The day's events did not turn on cracked crab. And yet it is precisely that fictitious crab that makes me see the afternoon all over again, a home movie run all too often, the father bearing gifts, the child weeping, an exercise in family love and guilt. Or that is what it was to me. Similarly, perhaps it never did snow that August in Vermont; perhaps there never were flurries in the night wind, and maybe no one else felt the ground hardening and summer already dead even as we pretended to bask in it, but that was how it felt to me, and it might as well have snowed, could have snowed, did snow.

*How it felt to me:* that is getting closer to the truth about a notebook. I sometimes delude myself about why I keep a notebook, imagine that

from *Slouching Towards Bethlehem*
by Joan Didion

*The real voyage of discovery consists not in seeking new landscapes, but in having new eyes.*

MARCEL PROUST

some thrifty virtue derives from preserving everything observed. See enough and write it down, I tell myself, and then some morning when the world seems drained of wonder, some day when I am only going through the motions of doing what I am supposed to do, which is write—on that bankrupt morning I will simply open my notebook and there it will all be, a forgotten account with accumulated interest, paid passage back to the world out there:...

I think we are well advised to keep on nodding terms with the people we used to be, whether we find them attractive company or not. Otherwise they turn up unannounced and surprise us, come hammering on the mind's door at 4 a.m. of a bad night and demand to know who deserted them, who betrayed them, who is going to make amends. We forget all too soon the things we thought we could never forget. We forget the loves and the betrayals alike, forget what we whispered and what we screamed, forget who we were. I have already lost touch with a couple of people I used to be; one of them, a seventeen-year-old, presents little threat, although it would be of some interest to me to know again what it feels like to sit on a river levee drinking vodka-and-orange-juice and listening to Les Paul and Mary Ford and their echoes sing "How High the Moon" on the car radio. (You see I still have the scenes, but I no longer perceive myself among those present, no longer could even improvise the dialogue.) The other one, a twenty-three-year old, bothers me more. She was always a good deal of trouble, and I suspect she will reappear when I least want to see her, skirts too long, shy to the point of aggravation, always the injured party, full of recriminations and little hurts and stories I do not want to hear again, at once saddening me and angering me with her vulnerability and ignorance, an apparition all the more insistent for being so long banished.

It is a good idea, then, to keep in touch, and I suppose that keeping in touch is what notebooks are all about. And we are all on our own when it comes to keeping those lines open to ourselves: your notebook will never help me, nor mine you.

*I always wanted to be somebody. I realize now that I should have been more specific.*

LILY TOMLIN

*When an inner situation is not made conscious, it appears outside as fate.*

C. G. JUNG

*Didion seems to see a "diary" as a factual record of daily events. What does she see as the purpose of a "notebook"?*

*What does she mean when she says that she sometimes tells lies in her notebooks?*

*She says a value for her of journaling is to "keep on nodding terms with the people we used to be." What might be some of the "parts" of you that you would like to stay in touch with over the years?*

*What do you see as the main purposes for keeping a journal?*

*What will most hinder and support you in keeping a regular journal for this seminar?*

As we explore who we are, it can be enjoyable and insightful to work with visual elements to create a self-portrait. We can then share our growing sense of who we are with others in the learning community and ask others what they see in our visual self-portrait.

## VISUAL SELF-REFLECTION

by Terry Sofianos and Paula Moscinski

Outside of class time consider the following questions: Who am I? What is important to me? Create a visual work that serves as your self-portrait at this present time. You may want to use photographs, copies of photographs, magazine pictures/text, paints, chalks, or any medium of your choosing. You may also consider using objects and creating a three-dimensional portrait. Use your imagination, go wild, and try not to get hung up on whether or not you're using "proper technique." Have fun! Be prepared to share these with our learning community.

Members of the community can provide feedback for each other. This can be in the form of notes to each other or comments. This feedback can be of assistance in creating your mission statement and/or getting closer to clarifying your values and/or passion.

You could also write in your journal about or share in a discussion of the following questions. This is to consciously bring forth the "gifts" that this self-reflection experience gave you.

*How did you form the idea for your portrait?*

*What was your process for deciding and acquiring the materials for the visual?*

*What was your creative process for putting it together?*

*What were you feeling/experiencing when you displayed it?*

*What was it like to give feedback on other's portraits?*

*What was it like to receive feedback on your portrait?*

*We are so many selves. It's not just the long-ago child within us who needs tenderness and inclusion, but the person we were last year, wanted to be yesterday, tried to become in one job or in one winter, in one love affair or in one house where even now, we can close our eyes and smell the rooms. What brings together these ever-shifting selves of infinite reactions and returnings is this: There is always one true inner voice. Trust it.*

GLORIA STEINEM, *REVOLUTION FROM WITHIN*

### JOURNALING PATTERNS

The following journaling activity invites a growing awareness and appreciation of the activities we most enjoy, the central passions of our life.

At the end of each day, briefly describe in your journal the one thing that you most loved doing during that day. Consider things you did at work or for leisure. Even if it seems insignificant, make note of it. Each day make your entry on a separate journal page. Don't skip a day. And don't reread other entries. After doing this for a period of time, look back at all of your entries. Look for patterns. Maybe you had a lot of entries that involved physical activity or music. Make a list of the different areas and notice the one in which you were involved the most times. These patterns and categories can lead you to identifying or clarifying your passions in life.

## GIVING AND RECEIVING FEEDBACK

The ability to provide constructive feedback to others is an important skill to develop. It is also important to develop an ability to effectively receive and utilize feedback given to you. Feedback, whether giving or receiving, involves a great deal of reflection. This will ensure that the feedback experience is meaningful. Following are some general principles that are helpful to keep in mind when giving and receiving feedback.

When giving feedback, it is important to remember to find out and respond to the receiver's concerns, speak for yourself only without assuming others' perceptions, avoid evaluative judgements and personal opinion, be specific, and help the receiver figure out how to act on your feedback.

When receiving feedback, it is important to remember to relax, be specific about the feedback you desire, listen carefully and be open to what is said, and clarify your understanding of the feedback by paraphrasing for the one giving it.

It may be easier to begin by evaluating past projects of students not currently enrolled in class. This will assist us in being able to be honest, as we often get too caught up in not wanting to upset others. It must be noted that it is important to continue developing your skills so that you can be both honest and diplomatic when there is a responsibility to interact with the person whose work you are evaluating.

Here is a possible format for the feedback process. We will work in small groups.

**Understanding of Purpose:** Group members will review the purpose and requirements of the project or assignment.

**Examination of Work:** Each project will be examined by each group member who will take notes on both strengths and weaknesses. Focus will be on the work and how well it achieves the purpose as understood.

**Warm Feedback:** Each group member will have an opportunity to comment on the strengths of the work.

**Cool Feedback:** Each group member will have an opportunity to comment on the weaknesses of the work including actions that could be taken to strengthen the work.

**Final Evaluation:** Group members will report to the class the project that they feel best meets the intent of the assignment and why. They may also comment on other things that stood out as they evaluated the projects.

*We don't see things as they are, we see them as we are.*

ANAÏS NIN

# unit four
# passion

*Objective: Identify personal passions and what role those passions may play in the future.*

**FLOW**

**EXCERPT FROM FLOW**

**PERSONAL FLOW QUESTIONNAIRE**

**YOUR HEART SONG**

**EXCERPT FROM LISTENING FOR THE DEEPER MUSIC**

**MUSIC THAT RESONATES WITH YOUR HEART SONG**

**DESCRIBING YOUR HEART SONG**

**PROSE, POETRY, AND PASSION**

**EXCERPT FROM THE TEACHINGS OF DON JUAN**

**THE LAST HOURS**

**THE JOURNEY**

**POETRY**

**PASSION MAPPING**

**PASSION PAPER**

**PASSION PAPER SAMPLES**

**PASSION PAPER WORKSHOP**

# PASSION

*Objective: Identify personal passions and what role those passions may play in the future.*

*The most beautiful things in the world cannot be seen or even touched. They must be felt with the heart.*

HELEN KELLER

Passion is the fuel for our life. It is what gets us out of bed every morning. But what ignites the flame of passion for each of us is very individual and unique. We must discover our passions and cultivate them throughout our lives.

Passion can be uncovered in participating in activities that we love. Perhaps we play basketball every chance we get. Or perhaps we turn to our easel and paints several times a day. Perhaps writing is our constant companion. Gardening may be a realm in which we "lose" and find ourselves. Or cooking. Or dancing. Or swimming. Or reading.

Passion can also be uncovered in ways we like to be. Perhaps being of service is something that lights our days. Perhaps being surrounded by nature feeds our soul. Perhaps being full of laughter gives us the fuel to travel through our days. Or being a leader. Or being a skilled communicator. Or being a nurturer for young children. Or being an adventurer.

Once we are clearly in tune with our passions we can create within our lives opportunities to participate in and express those passions. Oftentimes allowing our passions to lead the way creates the experience of flow. We lose track of time and savor every moment. The more we can live in passion and create flow within our lives, the more joy we will experience.

Conversely, if we are not clear about our passions or are afraid to embrace them, our lives can feel empty with each moment plodding forth with unbearable heaviness. We may escape into realms that attempt to recreate the experience of true passion, but we will always return with a crash into reality.

**FLOW**

Author Mihaly Csikszentmihalyi is considered to be the expert on the experience of flow. His book *Flow: The Psychology of Optimal Experience* is considered to be the cornerstone of all that we know about the topic. If we understand the experience of flow and identify within our lives when we have experienced it, we can begin to shine a light on what some of our passions might be.

Csikszentmihalyi contends that there are a number of conditions that must be present within the experience of flow. These conditions include: having clear goals, immediate feedback, skills that match the challenges, deep concentration, forgetting other problems, control, disappearance of self-consciousness, altered sense of time, and the feeling that the experience is worth having for its own sake. He further contends that the flow experience occurs when both the challenge to us and the skill level required of us are high.

## Flow: The Psychology of Optimal Experience

excerpt from

by Mihaly Csikszentmihalyi

*In flow there is no need to reflect, because the action carries us forward as if by magic.*

MIHALY CSIKSZENTMIHALYI

The opposite state from the condition of psychic entropy is optimal experience. When the information that keeps coming into awareness is congruent with goals, psychic energy flows effortlessly. There is no need to worry, no reason to question one's adequacy. But whenever one does stop to think about oneself, the evidence is encouraging: "You are doing all right." The positive feedback strengthens the self, and more attention is freed to deal with the outer and the inner environment.

Another one of our respondents, a worker named Rico Medellin, gets this feeling quite often on his job. He works in the same factory as Julio, a little further up on the assembly line. The task he has to perform on each unit that passes in front of his station should take forty-three seconds to perform—the same exact operation almost six hundred times in a working day. Most people would grow tired of such work very soon. But Rico has been at this job for over five years, and he still enjoys it. The reason is that he approaches his task in the same way an Olympic athlete approaches his event: How can I beat my record? Like the runner who trains for years to shave a few seconds off his best performance on the track, Rico has trained himself to better his time on the assembly line. With the painstaking care of a surgeon, he has worked out a private routine for how to use his tools, how to do his moves. After five years, his best average for a day has been twenty-eight seconds per unit. In part he tries to improve his perform-ance to earn a bonus and the respect of his supervisors. But most often he does not even let on to others that he is ahead and lets his success pass unnoticed. It is enough to know that he can do it, because when he is working at top performance the experience is so enthralling that it is almost painful for him to slow down. "It's better than anything else," Rico says. "It's a whole lot better than watching TV." Rico knows that very soon he will reach the limit beyond which he will no longer be able to improve his performance at his job. So twice a week he takes evening courses in electronics. When he has his diploma he will seek a more complex job, one that presumably he will confront with the same enthusiasm he has shown so far.

For Pam Davis it is much easier to achieve this harmonious, effortless state when she works. As a young lawyer in a small partnership, she is fortunate to be involved in complex, challenging cases. She spends hours in the library, chasing down references and outlining possible courses of action for the senior partners of the firm to follow. Often her concentration is so intense that she forgets to have lunch, and by the time she realizes that she is hungry it is dark outside. While she is immersed in her job every piece of information fits: even when she is temporarily frustrated, she knows what causes the frustrations, and she believes that eventually the obstacle can be overcome.

These examples illustrate what we mean by optimal experience. They are situations in which attention can be freely invested to achieve a person's goals, because there is no disorder to straighten out, no threat for the self to defend against. We have called this state the *flow experience,* because this is the term many of the people we interviewed had used in their descriptions of how it felt to be in top form: "It was like floating," "I was carried on by the flow." It is the opposite of psychic entropy—in fact, it is sometimes called negentropy—and those who attain it develop a stronger, more confident self, because more of their psychic energy has been invested successfully in goals they themselves had chosen to pursue.

When a person is able to organize his or her consciousness so as to experience flow as often as possible, the quality of life is inevitably going to improve, because, as in the case of Rico and Pam, even the usually boring routines of work become purposeful and enjoyable. In flow we are in control of our psychic energy, and everything we do adds order to consciousness. One of our respondents, a well-known West Coast rock climber, explains concisely the tie between the avocation that gives him a profound sense of flow and the rest of his life: "It's exhilarating to come closer and closer to self-discipline. You make your body go and everything hurts; then you look back in awe at the self, at what you've done, it just blows your mind. It leads to ecstasy, to self-fulfillment. If you win these battles enough, that battle against yourself, at least for a moment, it becomes easier to win the battles in the world."

*Breaking out is following your bliss pattern,*

*quitting the old place, starting your hero journey,*

*following your bliss.*

JOSEPH CAMPBELL

*What allows Rico Medellin to stay interested in a job that could start to feel mechanical very quickly?*

*What's the relationship between flow and psychic energy?*

*What does the author see as some of the main benefits of flow?*

*Csikszentmihalyi sees flow as a somewhat self-conscious and directed experience. Has this been your perception?*

# PERSONAL FLOW QUESTIONNAIRE

*How do you know you're having an experience of flow?*

*What activities most readily and consistently put you in flow?*

*Is it easier for you to get into flow with others or alone? When have you experienced either?*

*What factors, internal or external, most inhibit your experience of flow?*

*Do deadlines help or hinder your experience of flow?*

*It was easier for most people to get into flow as children. Why is that?*

*What do you personally most value about the flow experience?*

## YOUR HEART SONG

Musician Michael Jones writes eloquently in the article "Listening for the Deeper Music In Our Life and Work" of discovering and honoring the deep passions of our lives. Through reading and contemplating his words, we can further explore our own passions.

# Listening for the Deeper Music
## In Our Life and Work

by Michael Jones
from *Spirit At Work* newsletter
edited by Judi Neal, May 1998

*Live from your own center.*

JOSEPH CAMPBELL

As a pianist and composer, I can explain everything about a musical composition except the part that really matters. Yet it is the part that really matters that makes the difference between a composition that works and one that doesn't. This 'something other' cannot be mapped, analyzed, measured or weighed. It is like an invisible and emergent field that envelops me and the piano and the listener as I play. This informing spirit originates not in me or in the piano but in the space in between. And I do not go to it, it comes to me. While it seems perfectly ordinary when it is there, it seems impossible to find and hold when it is not. It comes to all of us in different ways. I feel it first in the quality of touch. It is like a tactile sensation in my fingers as they contact the piano keys. Then I hear details in the thematic development and rhythmic patterns that went unnoticed before. My fingers seem to merge with the instrument, passages which would have been technically impossible a few moments before are executed with greater ease as my fingers fall more lightly into the keys. Instead of striking or forcing the notes I sink into and mold or shape them as I play. With this new found ease, my hands now take the lead and suggest where the music goes next. They do so with an inner necessity and purposefulness that leaves little doubt that they know what they are doing. This is not noodling as my piano teachers of the past once suggested.

On the contrary, I believe that when I am willing to open a space to explore the music's ever changing form, I am creating an opportunity for another aspect of intelligence—like an experience that has been invisibly enfolded into the notes—to emerge. When this occurs, the roles between the left and right hand become more transparent, neither one tries to dominate the other. Instead each instinctively seems to know how to complement and add to what has gone before. When this happens, it feels like I am no longer playing with two hands, but with four. The challenge here is to be porous enough to not inhibit the flow or allow the fear that takes hold when I feel this much out of control to let me escape into a structure or analysis, because this pulls the life out of the music each time. In this respect it helps to remember the words of a jazz guitarist who, in speaking of his experience, said simply; "It is a particular kind of love."

My first encounter with this experience came as a child one day when I was playing with a set of replicas of tin soldiers with my friends. As they lined up their infantrymen and horse mounted cavalry, I created the sound track for it all. Suddenly, in a moment of self forgetfulness, I experienced what T. S. Eliot spoke of as the exhilaration and terror of that 'awful daring of a moment's surrender'. The piano was no longer a collection of strings and pins and wood, it was alive, for a brief instant I could not tell whether I was playing the piano, or it was playing me. As soon as I tried to analyze it, it was gone. In the years that followed, I became an apprentice to a set of practices that helped evoke this field and hold it. I also learned that these practices had less to do with talent or technique but with cultivating a certain sensitivity, a way of being that became a way of living a life.

The great American poet William Stafford found his way in by following what he described as 'the golden string'. William Stafford wrote a poem each day. When asked by poet Robert Bly how he accomplished such a remarkable output of poetry he replied, "I lowered my standards."

By this he meant that he did not wait for the 'right' impulse to come along, but took notice of whatever was immediately close at hand. Through following and enhancing that, the golden string led him into the poem. For Stafford, whatever he noticed was significant and therefore worthy of his attention. He had absolute faith in the authority of the golden string to lead him in. It knew where it was going, his work was to follow it without imposing his will or getting in the way. Being obedient to and trusting this impulse is an essential part of creating the ground for this 'something other' to emerge. It means not being too ambitious or goal driven or pulling too hard or the thread will break. Instead William Stafford adopted a neutral and trusting stance, including a willingness to welcome open-heartedly whatever came, whether they be thoughts, feelings, sounds, images, and impressions. His work was to maintain a state of readiness because he could not foresee what was about to enter into his field of awareness nor what he would be called upon to do. All he knew was not to resist these nudges, even if following this trail of emerging meaning did not mean much at the time, it would take him somewhere important if he just hung on. What was essential was to follow and trust its lead even if it seemed to be leading him into a dead end.

The 'Heaven's Gate' we are being led to is not necessarily fame or fortune or superior insight or even greater serenity. It is an awareness of our own true nature and an appreciation of that which is most centrally ours to do. "Who are you really, wanderer?" William Stafford asks in his poem, "What If It Were True." Is this towards the awareness of this deep purposefulness of life and to the riches it holds that this thread we are following eventually leads.

## Who Will Play Your Music?

Shortly after college, where I had majored in music and psychology, I left piano to develop a career as a consultant and educator. I did this for many years, playing the piano only for myself and a few friends when the occasion called for it. But through all this time I stayed close to the question of how to bring the music back into the center of my life. And I waited. It was only in hindsight that I discovered how much the consulting work served as a cover for the music to develop quietly and without my interruption.

Fifteen years passed this way until one evening during a management seminar in a small hotel, when an older man approached me as I played quietly for myself and after a brief conversation, asked pointedly; "Who will play your music, if you don't play it yourself?"

That question was a defining moment in my life. He had heard me in a way that gave me the courage-and permission-to bring the music fully into my life, even though I had very little idea where this commitment might lead. Several years later an unsolicited phone call led to an introduction and I became the founding artist with the newly formed Narada Records. The visit with the old man led me to wonder; is it possible that when another truly hears and gives voice to our dream–seeing in it a possibility greater than that which we hold for ourselves–they are setting free an energy that enables this promise to be fulfilled in the world.

When the questions themselves trouble us, it is not because they are too large, but because they are too small. When we are living the real questions, the ones that really matter to us, and which we deeply care about, the answers become less important. We come to love the question for itself because it has set us on a trail of emergent meaning that is giving us back our life. The journey becomes the goal. We don't want the inquiry to end too soon.

To participate in the world in this way means living a life which is more improvised than planned. By setting aside our repertoire we create the ground for new perspectives and insights to emerge. In this spirit of openness and curiosity we begin to find the end of the golden thread that will lead us in. Following this lead without resistance becomes the key that unlocks the door to the longing for home that rests deep within each heart. Nourish the longing, the Sufi Poet Kabir once said: "For it is the intensity of the longing that does all the work."

The longing leads us to our own truth, a truth which we discover is not a concept which is fixed or solid, but a feeling that changes as we engage with the unfolding reality of our own life. This is our songline-a songline of the heart. To follow our songline is an act of great faith because our heart will often lead us in directions contrary to what our logic would suggest. As we listen to and respect its direction with innocent eyes and innocent ears, a stillness comes upon us–we are present now in the emergent field of being. In this moment our life feels that it has just begun even as our long journey into it is not perhaps complete.

## Closing Thoughts

Each of us possesses a unique quality of perception and experience which is our own truth, one that cannot be expressed by anyone else but ourselves. When William Stafford asks, "Who are you really, wanderer?" he is inviting us to go down into the very marrow of our life. What awaits us there is the realization that we belong not only to organizations and careers, but also to a story, the mythic proportions of which is unfolding whether we are aware of its legacy in our life or not.

## References

*The Darkness Around Us Is Deep*, Selected Poems of William Stafford, edited with an introduction by Robert Bly. Harper Perennial. 1993
*Songlines*, Bruce Chatwin, Penguin, 1987
*The Essential Jesus; Original Sayings and Earliest Images*, John Dominic Crossan, Harper Collins, 1994.

*Jones speaks about an experience he first had as a child (when he played with a set of toy soldiers), which later returned whenever he would have a truly "creative" moment. How does he describe these moments and in what ways are they familiar to you?*

*What role does Jones feel the imagination plays in creating these "moments of surrender"? What is your sense of what allows these moments to happen?*

*Jones talks about listening for the deeper questions. What are some of the deeper questions that keep resurfacing in your life, especially now?*

*Jones describes a "defining moment" when an older man, having heard him playing the piano, approaches him and asks, "Who will play your music, if you don't play it yourself?" Have you had a "defining moment" in terms of your "deeper music"?*

*In pursuing one's deeper music, Jones quotes the Sufi poet Kabir, who says, "For it is the intensity of the longing that does all the work." What is it that your heart truly longs to do in this life?*

*It don't mean a thing if you ain't got that swing.*

DUKE ELLINGTON AND IRVING MILLS

*Music is your own experience, your thoughts, your wisdom. If you don't live it, it won't come out of your horn.*

CHARLIE PARKER

## MUSIC THAT RESONATES WITH YOUR HEART SONG

If you were to pick any piece of music that you know, what piece would most resonate with your own heart song and why? If you'd like, you can bring it to class and share it with the community.

## DESCRIBING YOUR HEART SONG

Michael Jones speaks about a defining moment that occurs when the older man, a total stranger, asks him, "Who will play your music, if you don't play it yourself?" This "deeper music" is our "spirit gift," what we have that is special and unique to offer up to the world. It could be a quality, a talent, a sensitivity, a passion; it is what makes us feel most alive, happy, and fulfilled. To help you begin exploring the question "What is my spirit gift, my life passion?" reflect on your own "deeper music." Let the metaphor remain somewhat vague and intuitive, more a "felt sense" than a direct meaning. How would you express your "heart song"? Some questions to consider might be:

*What color is your heart song?*

*What style is it in? (blues, classical, punk, opera, what?)*

*What instrument(s) would play it?*

*What mood(s) or feeling(s) would you want to evoke?*

*What would the song be about?*

*To whom, for whom, would you be playing/singing your song?*

# Inspired by your journal writing, now describe your heart song.

Let your imagination and intuition lead the way. Listen to your heart more than to your mind. Express your heart song in words, images, sound, movement, whatever feels most direct and true for you. You can even sing it if you like. Please describe or express your own heart song rather than playing a song someone else has written. You'll share this heart song with the learning community.

*If you want to identify me, ask me not where I live, or what I like to eat, or how I comb my hair, but ask me what I am living for, in detail, and ask me what I think is keeping me from living fully for the thing I want to live for.*

THOMAS MERTON

## PROSE, POETRY, AND PASSION

Creative artists are driven by passion just as we all are. Poets and creative writers use their talents to put in writing very poignant expressions of passion and its place in our lives. In this excerpt from *The Teachings of Don Juan* by Carlos Castaneda, the author asks if there is a special way to avoid pain. Don Juan responds.

# the teachings
excerpt from

of Don Juan

by Carlos Castaneda

" The devil's weed is only one of a million paths. Anything is one of a million paths [un camino entre cantidades de caminos]. Therefore you must always keep in mind that a path is only a path; if you feel you should not follow it, you must not stay with it under any conditions. To have such clarity you must lead a disciplined life. Only then will you know that any path is only a path, and there is no affront, to oneself or to others, in dropping it if that is what your heart tells you to do. But your decision to keep on the path or to leave it must be free of fear or ambition. I warn you. Look at every path closely and deliberately. Try it as many times as you think necessary. This question is one that only a very old man asks. My benefactor told me about it once when I was young, and my blood was too vigorous for me to understand it. Now I do understand it. I will tell you what it is: Does this path have a heart? All paths are the same: they lead nowhere. They are paths going through the bush, or into the bush. In my own life I could say I have traversed long, long paths, but I am not anywhere. My benefactor's question has meaning now. Does this path have a heart? If it does, the path is good; if it doesn't, it is of no use. Both paths lead nowhere; but one has a heart, the other doesn't. One makes for a joyful journey; as long as you follow it, you are one with it. The other will make you curse your life. One makes you strong; the other weakens you."

*We must be willing to get rid of the life we've*

*planned, so as to have the life that is waiting for us.*

JOSEPH CAMPBELL

*In* The Teachings of Don Juan, *Carlos Castaneda describes a "path with heart" and what's involved in choosing, taking, or not taking one. What most stands out for you in his description?*

*Have you found your path with heart yet? If so, what is it? If not, why not?*

*Is it possible to have more than one path with heart at the same time? Can a path with heart evolve into something different over time?*

# the last
# HOURS

There's some innocence left,
and these are the last hours of an empty afternoon
at the office, and there's the clock
on the wall, and my friend Frank
in the adjacent cubicle selling himself
on the phone.
        I'm twenty-five, on the shaky
ladder up, my father's son, corporate,
clean-shaven, and I know only what I don't want,
which is almost everything I have.
        A meeting ends.
Men in serious suits, intelligent men
who've been thinking hard about marketing snacks,
move back now to their window offices, worried
or proud. The big boss, Horace,
had called them into approve this, reject that—
the big boss, a first-name, how's—your—family
kind of assassin, who likes me.
        It's 1964.
The sixties haven't begun yet. Cuba is a larger name
than Vietnam. The Soviets are behind
everything that could be wrong. Where I sit
it's exactly nineteen minutes to five. My phone rings.
Horace would like me to stop in
before I leave. Stop in. Code words,
leisurely words, that mean *now.*
        Would I be willing
to take on this? Would X's office, who by the way
is no longer with us, be satisfactory?
About money, will this be enough?
I smile, I say yes and yes and yes,
but—I don't know from what calm place
this comes—I'm translating
his beneficence into a lifetime, a life
of selling snacks, talking snack strategy,
thinking snack thoughts.
        On the elevator down
it's a small knot, I'd like to say, of joy.
That's how I tell it now, here in the future,
the fear long gone.
By the time I reach the subway it's grown,
it's outsized, an attitude finally come round,
and I say it quietly to myself, *I quit,*
and keep saying it, knowing I will say it, sure
of nothing else but.

by Stephen Dunn
from *Different Hours*

One day you finally knew
what you had to do, and began,
though the voices around you
kept shouting
their bad advice—
though the whole house
began to tremble
and you felt the old tug
at your ankles.
"Mend my life!"
each voice cried.
But you didn't stop.
You knew what you had to do,
though the wind pried
with its stiff fingers
at the very foundations,
though their melancholy
was terrible.
It was already late
enough, and a wild night,
and the road full of fallen
branches and stones.
But little by little,
as you left their voices behind,
the stars began to burn
through the sheets of clouds,
and there was a new voice
which you slowly
recognized as your own,
that kept you company
as you strode deeper and deeper
into the world,
determined to do
the only thing you could do—
determined to save
the only life you could save.

the
Journey
by Mary Oliver

# poetry

And it was at that age…Poetry arrived
in search of me. I don't know, I don't know where
it came from. from winter or a river.
I don't know how or when,
no, they were not voices, they were not
words, nor silence,
but from a street I was summoned,
from the branches of night,
abruptly from the others,
among violent fires
or returning alone,
there I was without a face
and it touched me.

I did not know what to say, my mouth
had no way
with names,
my eyes were blind,
and something started in my soul,
fever or forgotten wings,
and I made my own way,
deciphering
that fire,
and I wrote the first faint line,
faint, without substance, pure
nonsense,
pure wisdom
of someone who knows nothing,
and suddenly I saw
the heavens
unfastened
and open,
planets,
palpitating plantations,
shadow perforated,
riddled
with arrows, fire and flowers,
the winding night, the universe.

And I, infinitesimal being,
drunk with the great starry
void,
likeness, image of
mystery,
I felt myself a pure part
of the abyss,
I wheeled with the stars,
My heart broke loose on the wind.

by Pablo Neruda
translated by Alastair Reid

*In reading the three poems, "The Last Hours," "The Journey," and "Poetry," what do each of the poems tell us about the process and consequences of discovering and walking one's path with heart?*

*Which poem are you most drawn to? Why do you think that is?*

*Mary Oliver speaks of "the only thing you could do." What do you feel right now is "the only thing you [can] do"? How do you know that? How will you make sure that you will do it?*

*Pablo Neruda writes, "My heart broke loose on the wind." When have you experienced this feeling? What were you doing? Do you experience this feeling often? Why or why not?*

*"The Journey" and "Poetry" share many similarities. How does the poem "The Last Hours" differ from them? How is it similar?*

*"The Last Hours"—of what?*

*Have you shared an experience similar to the one described by Stephen Dunn? What was that like?*

## PASSION MAPPING

This activity will be a creative tool for preparing you to write your passion paper. You may choose the method (conceptual or chronological) that seems most interesting for you.

Choose paper and writing materials. The more creative, the materials the better (construction paper, large paper, markers, crayons, pastels, paints). Work with your paper horizontally. Use mostly symbols and images as you work, with occasional words.

As you work creatively, feel free to listen to music, preferably without lyrics.

Throughout the experience, notice what creative elements are arising that would not have been present in a traditional outlining experience (the significance of the colors and symbols you choose can enlighten you to hidden aspects of your connection to your passion).

Use your map to create an outline for your paper. Include metaphors you discovered in mapping ("I used a lot of red, which indicates the depth of my passion," "The image of a key crystallizes how I feel about my life").

### Conceptual Map

Contemplate and then draw a symbol/image representing yourself (guitar, lightbulb, film camera, theater masks—or more complex, abstract images). The image should be drawn in the center of the paper.

When your central image is complete, create branches representing each of your main passions in life. Be creative with your branches (tree limbs, lightning bolts, flower stems, curves, angles). Label each branch.

When the branches are filled in and labeled, fill in smaller branches for details about each of the passions: how it started, who supported it, your vision for its future in your life, obstacles.

Work creatively, filling the paper with meaningful color, image, and words.

### Chronological Map

Create an image somewhere on your paper representing your birth.

Begin drawing a path representing your life's journey.

Fill in images and words that represent defining moments along your journey (people, events, passions).

Work creatively, filling the paper with meaningful color, image, and words.

*The events in our lives happen in a sequence in time, but in their significance to ourselves, they find their own order...the continuous thread of revelation.*

EUDORA WELTY

*We get to a certain age, and then the rest of our lives we do everything we can to get back to the way we were when we were little....using wisdom to come back to innocence.*

KATE BUSH

## PASSION PAPER

We've been looking at passion, purpose, and values as they are expressed in our lives. We've explored talents and gifts, flow experiences, and experiences of success. We've more closely considered how passions can come in the form of an activity or a way of being or a common thread that runs through many activities in our lives. Considering all of these elements, what would you say are your main creative passions in life at the present time? Contemplating these passions, write a paper using the guidelines that follow.

You may use your passion map, created in the last activity, to spark ideas. You can create an outline from your passion map. You can include metaphors you discovered in mapping ("I used a lot of red, which indicates the depth of my passion," "The image of a key crystallizes how I feel about my life"). Whether you refer to your passion map or not, outlining is the first step to a coherent paper.

Make sure that you write authentically. This paper is about you. Consider including favorite quotes (from poems, books, songs).

Use the following format:

**Title:** Choose a title that crystallizes the essence of your paper in a meaningful way.

**Introduction:** Explain what passion means to you and why it matters in your life.

### Body (Part One): My Passions; Past Reflections
Identify two to three passions that have been significant in your life. For each of these, tell the history of how it developed, including its origins, its key expressions or experiences, support for its development (including people, events, values), challenges of its development (including people and events), and how you dealt with those challenges. Be as concrete and detailed as, possible including specific stories and anecdotes.

### Body (Part Two): My Passions; Future Intentions
How do you envision including these passions in your future life (including your work, relationships, and activities)? What do you need to do now to ensure that that happens?

**Conclusion:** Write a powerful, motivational summary of your thoughts.

## PASSION PAPER SAMPLES

The following excerpt is from a passion paper written by a student. This is a good example of a paper that expresses an abstract passion.

excerpt from
# communicating my
# PASSION

My main creative passion in life is the art of communication. I intensely study the way humans are, and how my actions, words, and constructions influence others; how other people's actions, words, and constructions influence others. I find life intriguing and I find that my passion lies in the connections that bond life forms together.

I am a marketing major. I am not in it for the money. I am in it because I am passionate about communication and everything included in that. I am passionate about the way that mini vans are designed. I am passionate about the lingo of fifth graders. I am passionate about knowing the right thing to say to make someone smile. I desire to master the art of communication.

Thinking back to the earliest memory I have of becoming conscious of this passion takes place when I was about five or six years old. My mother would make a special trip to buy milk from this deli near our house. She would drive up and send me in by myself with exactly enough money to buy one gallon of milk. It was the first store I ever went in by myself, and the first time I ever dealt with the cashier.

Kate Alpert
2000

I remember buying milk there many times, but on one occasion there was a horribly miserable old lady working behind the counter. She was big and mean and she looked like she had never smiled in her whole life. I decided I would smile at her to see how she would react. I walked up to the counter.

"One gallon of two percent," I said. I gave the lady a smile and I looked her right in the eyeballs like she was the most beautiful woman I had ever seen in my life. She froze for a moment then smiled back at me. She went from being angry and ugly to being proud and glowing. She smiled back at me and said "thank you." It was genuine.

That experience made me understand that a person's mood could be shifted with simply a look. I saw how much power words have. And even more how much power a smile has. Looking back that was the moment that seems to have started my passion for communication.

The following excerpt is from a passion paper written by a student. This is a good example of a paper that expresses a concrete passion.

excerpt from

# Acting,
## THE
# Passion
# FRUIT
## That Hangs in my Soul

One of my best friends is in acting school with me right now and he has become disenchanted with the craft. He got a great job at a bar, and it is clouding his thoughts. The thing that gets me, is the fact that he is a wonderful actor. His range of talent is incredible. It makes me sad to see him go through this. I can't do anything for him to get him acting again. The thing with being an artist is all in personal choices. You have to really want to be an actor one-hundred percent of the time, and your heart has to be in it. If you aren't committed totally to the craft, then the final product is going to be false. I have always felt that my job as an actor is to become a vessel for the playwright's work and present it as truthfully as I can in the set imaginary circumstances of the play. I'm at a point with acting, where I've been doing it so long, that I can see how someone could get disenchanted with it. There are many people in the acting world who piss you off on a daily basis so much that you could say, to hell with it, and join the business world in three seconds flat. What keeps me going is the purity of the craft. In every single thing you do in your life there are going to be obstacles and stupid people who make a mockery of what you do. I say forget them and stay gold.

Right now I just want to act, read, and possibly write when I have the time. A relationship would be a nice additive, too. I want to make new relationships with directors, actors, and other artists. Right now, I don't see a wife and family in the picture. Down the road, maybe. I love opening night, sharing my work with anyone who will listen. I love the smell and feel of the theater. The sound your feet make as you make your first entrance in a new play. I love the way I can see the audience out of my peripheral view while I'm onstage. I love how they react when I do something right or funny. Making someone laugh is like nothing else in the world. Making their whole body rivet in enthusiastic pleasure makes me respond the same way. Just making the audience respond is enough to make me smile, but the real reward is seeing that the audience really interpreted the play. Then I know I've done my job as an actor and that is satisfying. When I'm done with a show and someone says to me "God, I hated you, but I cried for you at the end," that is what this craft is all about, and it is why I put every part of my being into manufacturing it every day. If I'm not involved in a play, I don't feel right. I feel incomplete. It is the constant yearning for more and more artistic investment in a project that really lets an actor breathe. Most of us smoke too much anyway. At this point in time, my utmost love is acting. Everything else comes second. This philosophy has hurt me in my life. I don't care. Acting is my art, my chaos, my love, and it is what I want to do till the day I die.

Garrett Matheson
2002

# PASSION PAPER WORKSHOP

This workshop is to support and encourage you to express the story of your passion as clearly and inspirationally as possible. From a place of nonjudgment and goodwill, with a partner, you will read and listen to each other's papers. (Be sure to make a photocopy for your partner so they can follow along as you read.) Comments will be both spoken and written. Consider these comments from classmates not as criticisms but rather as gifts of insight that will assist in finding your voice and telling your truth. You will create a sense of small group community through "serving" each other in this way.

With a partner, take turns reading your passion papers aloud to each other. While your partner is reading their paper aloud, read along, marking on your copy any thoughts, questions, and so on that occur to you. Include references to things you like, where things feel unclear or awkward, where you would like things developed or want more details, and where it feels like the flow breaks or there is a disconnect. As you read your own paper aloud, you yourself can note places where you stumbled, got lost, or wished you had explained more.

When your partner has finished reading their paper aloud, you can give them feedback based on the notes you took. Share with your partner what most stands out for you about their paper, the most striking section and why it is most striking, anything that feels missing from the paper, whether or not there is a consistency between the voice of the text and the voice of the reader as we've gotten to know him/her, whether or not there is a strong conclusion, well considered and thought provoking.

# Following the feedback session, you both can read the paper silently and make notes on the paper regarding the form and structure of the writing:

*Organization (introduction, body, conclusion, transitions)*

*Paragraph structure*

*Sentence structure (run-ons, subject/verb agreement, fragments)*

*Misspellings*

*Typos*

*Tense errors*

*Voicing errors (for example, switching from first to third person)*

*Unclear or redundant language*

If you wish, you may write a letter of your impressions/suggestions at the end of the copy of the paper, sign it, and return it to your partner. Complete this process for both partners.

# chapter 2

## SERVING COMMUNITY

| objective | | outcome | readings | other elements |
|---|---|---|---|---|
| **unit 1** | Develop an understanding of and appreciation for our communities. | Students will identify their current communities.<br>Students will contemplate the relationship between happiness and community involvement.<br>Students will explore the ways in which community bonds are strengthened. | *Bowling Alone* | Community Potluck<br>Community Mapping |
| **unit 2** | Understand the purpose and experience of service. | Students will review past experiences with serving and messages about service from family and society.<br>Students will read about service and perform acts of service, learning to distinguish between serving, fixing, and helping.<br>Students will examine how others have experienced the rewards and challenges of service. | *Engaging the Next Generation*<br>Volunteering vs. Voting<br>*In the Service of Life*<br>*Start Small* | Random Acts of Service<br>Starting Small<br>Interviewing a Community<br>    Leader or Volunteer<br>Finding Inspiration in the Media |
| **unit 3** | Consider interests and skills in the process of identifying opportunities to serve. | Students will identify the most compelling communities, issues, and causes.<br>Students will identify their talents, skills, and resources.<br>Students will develop a list of opportunities to serve. | | Consider Your Options<br>The Service Lottery<br>Identify Your Interests<br>Identify Your Talents and Resources<br>Research Your Options<br>Put It All Together |
| **unit 4** | Plan and implement a group community service project and reflect on its impact. | While learning to be part of an effective team, students will carry out a group service project.<br>Students will reflect on the experience through writing and reading. | Building a Team<br>Community Service Papers<br>*Have a Heart and Give to a Young Heart* | How to Choose a Group Project<br>Compass Points<br>Community Service Preparation<br>    Checklist<br>Reflecting On Our Service<br>    Experience<br>Documenting the Service Project |

**SERVING COMMUNITY**

*Everyone has the power for greatness, not for fame but for greatness, because greatness is determined by service.*

MARTIN LUTHER KING JR.

The mission of Columbia College is to prepare students to "author the culture of their times." To do this, you need more than technical ability. We need compassion, clarity of vision, an understanding of community, the creativity that comes from listening to one's inner voice, and the wisdom that emerges from listening to and collaborating with others.

How do we become more engaged in the community and author a culture that embodies our highest ideals? How do we see the light in others and be the light that we have seen? Senior Seminar encourages you to deepen your understanding of yourself and each other and to explore the ways in which service can be part of a rewarding and meaningful life. Through discussions, readings, watching videos, and interacting with guest speakers, you encounter people who followed their inner voices, who addressed problems in community and society, and who experienced the joy of service.

Citizens, activists, and artists of all disciplines have used their skills to address important issues in society. Every community and every medium offer opportunities for us to address important issues and to serve one another. Although one doesn't typically think of dance as a social engineering discipline, Liz Lehrman is a dancer and choreographer who communicates about human and community issues such as aging and cultural diversity in her work. As an actress and writer, Anna Deveare Smith has used her work to address issues ranging from the riots in Los Angeles to racial diversity in New York City. Tony Kushner is an example of someone in the theater community who has used his work to explore a variety of social and human rights issues, particularly relating to the gay community.

Students in Senior Seminar have used their skills and talents to produce audiotapes and make hand puppets for children in a refugee camp in Croatia; to take walks, sing, and celebrate the holidays with residents of a nursing home; to organize an arts festival with proceeds benefiting charity; to create a song and dance about butterflies for children in a local day care center; to develop an advertising campaign for the Humane Society; and to create a time capsule with a kindergarten class. We may not be able to change the world, but we have seen that we can make a small difference in someone else's life. Above all, we have found that it makes us feel good to help others.

Serving a cause, an issue, a neighborhood, even one person, is a way to reach outside the self, to create a meaningful connection that shares our light with the world and gives us happiness. If each person could imagine a future in which our children are cherished, our environment is protected, our neighbors have roofs over their heads and food on their tables, our neighborhoods are peaceful, and our society is just, and then take responsibility for creating that future, we would each feel the joy of service and of living in a better world.

Why serve? There are many reasons to serve and many ways to serve. Some people look at service as an opportunity to further their spiritual awareness and development. They see service as a way to create a better world while making a positive deposit on their karmic balance sheet. Other people see service as a way to experience relatedness and closeness; they look for opportunities to serve in communities or in ways that bring them together with others. Still other people see service as a way to develop their professional skills. You may have the opportunity to perform a service as a volunteer—to create a mural, to produce a public interest campaign, to organize a fund-raising event, to design an annual report—that allows you to stretch and demonstrate your skills and to add an important credit to your resume. Finally, through service you may develop a sense of mission and meaning for your life. You may even find a worthwhile career.

During our semester together as a Senior Seminar learning community, the questions we raise are an integral part of our self-discovery: Have you recognized and appreciated the many ways that others have served you? Are you a net asset to the planet? Have you contributed more than the resources you have consumed? Each of us can incorporate a spirit of service into our lives, our families, our neighborhoods, and our work. In this unit on serving community are the activities and experiences that we use in Senior Seminar as we ask students to explore their hearts and their communities, to discuss and experience service, and to reflect on their service experience.

# WHAT YOU PASS ON

A couple of years ago I found out what "you can't take it with you" means. I found out while I was lying in a ditch at the side of a country road, covered with mud and blood and with the tibia of my right leg poking out the side of my jeans like the branch of a tree taken down in a thunderstorm. I had a MasterCard in my wallet, but when you're lying in a ditch with broken glass in your hair, no one accepts MasterCard.

We all know that life is ephemeral, but on that particular day and in the months that followed, I got a painful but extremely valuable look at life's simple backstage truths. We come in naked and broke. We may be dressed when we go out, but we're just as broke. Warren Buffet? Going to go out broke. Bill Gates? Going out broke. Tom Hanks? Going out broke. Steve King? Broke. Not a crying dime.

All the money you earn, all the stocks you buy, all the mutual funds you trade—all of that is mostly smoke and mirrors. It's still going to be a quarter-past getting late whether you tell the time on a Timex or a Rolex. No matter how large your bank account, no matter how many credit cards you have, sooner or later things will begin to go wrong with the only three things you have that you can really call your own: your body, your spirit and your mind.

So I want you to consider making your life one long gift to others. And why not? All you have is on loan, anyway. All that lasts is what you pass on.

Yes—charity begins at home. Those of you who pay for the college educations of your sons and daughters do a wonderful thing. If you're able to give them a further start in life—a place in business, help with a home—so much the better. Because charity *begins* at home. Because— up to a certain point, at least—we are all responsible for the lives we add to the world.

But I think the most chilling thing a young man or woman can hear is, "Someday all this will be yours." I think what a lot would *like* to hear is some version of, "You're on your own. Good luck. Call if you need help—and reverse the charges."

Now imagine a nice little backyard, surrounded by a board fence. Dad—a pleasant fellow, a little plump—is tending the barbecue. Mom

by Stephen King

*When we quit thinking primarily about ourselves and our own self-preservation, we undergo a truly heroic transformation of consciousness....The ultimate aim of the quest must be neither release nor ecstasy for oneself, but wisdom and power to serve others.*

JOSEPH CAMPBELL

and the kids are setting the picnic table: fried chicken, coleslaw, potato salad, a chocolate cake for dessert. And standing around the fence, looking in, are emaciated men and women, starving children. They are silent. They only watch.

That family at the picnic is us; that backyard is America, and those hungry people on the other side of the fence, watching us sit down to eat, include far too much of the rest of the world: Asia and the subcontinent; countries in Central Europe, where people live on the edge from one harvest to the next; South America, where they're burning down the rain forests; and most of all, Africa, where AIDS is pandemic and starvation is a fact of life.

It's not a pretty picture, but we have the power to help, the power to change. And why should we refuse? Because we're going to take it with us? Please.

Giving isn't about the receiver or the gift but the giver. It's *for* the giver. One doesn't open one's wallet to improve the world, although it's nice when that happens; one does it to improve one's self. I give because it's the only concrete way I have of saying that I'm glad to be alive and that I can earn my daily bread doing what I love. Giving is a way of taking the focus off the money we make and putting it back where it belongs—on the lives we lead, the families we raise, the communities that nurture us.

A life of giving—not just money, but time and spirit—repays. It helps us remember that we may be going out broke, but right now we're doing O.K. Right now we have the power to do great good for others and for ourselves.

So I ask you to begin giving, and to continue as you begin. I think you'll find in the end that you got far more than you ever had, and did more good than you ever dreamed.

*I am only one; but still I am one. I cannot do everything, but still I can do something. I will not refuse to do the something I can do.*

HELEN KELLER

*Stephen King came to a realization about life after being hit by a car and facing his own mortality. Have you had a similar epiphany or realization? What was the stimulus and what new awareness did you gain?*

*What great gifts or examples of generosity have you observed, received, and offered?*

*Which of King's ideas is the most meaningful or relevant for you? And why?*

*According to King, "Right now we have the power to do great good for others and for ourselves." Whom do you have the power to help? Where do you see an opportunity to give? What "great good" might you offer?*

# unit one
# exploring
## our communities

**EXCERPT FROM BOWLING ALONE**

**COMMUNITY POTLUCK**

**COMMUNITY MAPPING**

*Objective: Develop an understanding of and appreciation for our communities.*

A s we begin to think about service, we first consider our involvement in community and society. With which communities are we connected and in what ways do we experience community with one another? In our communities, our networks of community engagement, our bonds are formed by communication, cooperation, and mutual support. They are strengthened by our contributions, by our willingness to serve one another and to serve our highest ideals.

In *Bowling Alone* Robert Putnam notes the erosion of community in our lives, showing that past generations have been more involved in civic life and in helping others in the community. He challenges us with the thesis that "happiness is best predicted by the breadth and depth of one's social connections." In this unit, we will explore our connections to various communities, we will look for opportunities to strengthen our communities by sharing and serving, and we will study, experience and celebrate our community relationships.

# excerpt from Bowling Alone

by Robert Putnam

For the first two-thirds of the twentieth century a powerful tide bore Americans into ever deeper engagement in the life of their communities, but a few decades ago—silently, without warning—that tide reversed and we were overtaken by a treacherous rip current. Without at first noticing, we have been pulled apart from one another and from our communities over the last third of the century….

Thirty-two million fewer American adults were involved in community affairs in the mid-1990s than would have been involved at the proportional rate of two decades earlier….

In recent years social scientists have framed concerns about the changing character of American society in terms of the concept of "social capital." By analogy with notions of physical capital and human capital —tools and training that enhance individual productivity—the core idea of social capital theory is that social networks have value. Just as a screwdriver (physical capital) or a college education (human capital) can increase productivity (both individual and collective), so too social contacts affect the productivity of individuals and groups.

Whereas physical capital refers to physical objects and human capital refers to properties of individuals, social capital refers to connections among individuals—social networks and the norms of reciprocity and trustworthiness that arise from them In that sense social capital is closely related to what some have called "civic virtue." The difference is that "social capital" calls attention to the fact that civic virtue is most powerful when embedded in a dense network of reciprocal social relations. A society of many virtuous but isolated individuals is not necessarily rich in social capital. …

…Social capital has both an individual and a collective aspect—a private face and a public face. First, individuals form connections that benefit our own interests. One pervasive strategem of ambitious job seekers is "networking," for most of us get our jobs because of whom we know, not what we know—that is, our social capital, not our human capital. Economic sociologist Ronald Burt has shown that executives with bounteous Rolodex files enjoy faster career advancement. Nor is the private return to social capital limited to economic rewards.

As Claude S. Fischer, a sociologist of friendship, has noted, "Social networks are important in all our lives, often for finding jobs, more often for finding a helping hand, companionship, or a shoulder to cry on."[1]

If individual clout and companionship were all there were to social capital, we'd expect foresighted, self-interested individuals to invest the right amount of time and energy in creating or acquiring it. However, social capital also can have "externalities" that affect the wider community, so that not all the costs and benefits of social connections accrue to the person making the contact.[2]

⦿

… A well-connected individual in a poorly connected society is not as productive as a well-connected individual in a well-connected society. And even a poorly connected individual may derive some of the spillover benefits from living in a well-connected community. If the crime rate in my neighborhood is lowered by neighbors keeping an eye on one another's homes, I benefit even if I personally spend most of my time on the road and never even nod to another resident on the street.

Social capital can thus be simultaneously a "private good" and a "public good." Some of the benefit from an investment in social capital goes to bystanders, while some of the benefit redounds to the immediate interest of the person making the investment. …

⦿

Countless studies document the link between society and psyche: people who have close friends and confidants, friendly neighbors, and supportive co-workers are less likely to experience sadness, loneliness, low self-esteem, and problems with eating and sleeping. Married people are consistently happier than most people who are unattached, all else being equal. These findings will hardly surprise most Americans, for in study after study, people themselves report that good relationships with family members, friends or romantic partners—far more than money or fame—are prerequisites for their happiness.[3] The single most common finding from a half century's research on the correlates of life satisfaction, not only in the United States but around the world, is that happiness is best predicted by the breadth and depth of one's social connections.[4]

### Footnotes

[1] Ronald S. Burt, Structural Holes: The Social Structure of Competition (Cambridge, Mass.: Harvard University Press, 1992); Ronald S. Burt, " The Contingent Value of Social Capital," Administrative Science Quarterly 42 (1997): 339-365; and Ronald S. Burt, "The Gender of Social Capital," Rationality & Society 10 (1985): 5-46; Claude S. Fischer, "Network Analysis and Urban Studies," in Networks and Places: Social Relations in the Urban Setting, ed. Claude S. Fischer (New York: Free Press, 1977), 19; James D. Montgomery, "Social Networks and Labor-Market Outcomes: Toward an Economic Analysis," American Economic Review 81 (1991): 1408-1418, esp. table 1.

[2] In earlier work I emphasized this public dimension of social capital almost to the exclusion of the private returns to social capital. See Robert D. Putnam, "The Prosperous Community: Social Capital and Public Affairs," The American Prospect 143 (1993): 35-42, on which the present text draws. For a literature review that highlights the private returns almost to the exclusion of the collective dimension, see Alejandro Portes, "Social Capital: Its Origins and Applications in Modern Sociology," Annual Review of Sociology 22 (1998): 1-24.

[3] L.I. Pearlin, M.A. Lieberman, E.G. Menaghan, J.T. Mullan, "The Stress Process," Journal of Health and Social Behavior 22, no 4 (1981): 337-356; A. Billings and R. Moos, "Social Support and Functioning Among Community and Clinical Groups: A Panel Model," Journal of Behavioral Medicine 5, no 3 (1982): 295-311; G. A. Kaplan, R.E. Roberts, T.C. Camacho, and J.C. Coyne, "Psychosocial Predictors of Depression," American Journal of Epidemiology 125, no 2, (1987), 206-220; P. Cohen, E.L. Struening, G.L. Muhlin, L.E. Genevie, S.R. Kaplan, and H. B. Peck, "Community Stressors, Mediating Conditions and Well-being in Urban Neighborhoods," Journal of Community Psychology 10 (1982): 377-391; David G. Myers, "Close Relationships and Quality of Life," in D. Kahneman, E. Diener, and N. Schwartz, eds., Well-Being: The Foundations of Hedonic Psychology (New York: Russell Sage Foundation, 1999).

[4] Michael Argyle, The Psychology of Happiness (London: Metheun, 1987); Ed Diener, "Subjective Well-being," Psychological Bulletin 95 (1984): 542-575; Ed Diener, "Assessing Subjective Well-being," Social Indicators Research, 31 (1994): 103-157; David G. Myers and Ed Diener, "Who Is Happy?" Psychological Science 6 (1995): 10-19; Ruut Veenhoven, "Developments in Satisfaction-Research," Social Indicators Research, 37 (1996): 1-46; and works cited there.

## COMMUNITY POTLUCK: APPRECIATING CULTURAL DIFFERENCES

We can strengthen the relationships within our learning community by holding a community potluck and inviting each person to bring a dish that reflects his or her particular upbringing. This is a way to get to know each other better and to appreciate and savor our differences as a prelude to working together on a group service project. Before eating, we can introduce our dishes and talk about our cultural backgrounds and the flavor of the dinner table as we were growing up. We may find that we've never spent much time at a dinner table, what with both parents having to work and family members pursuing their individual interests. When this is the case, we may want to support each other in creating new dinner rituals with our friends and family. We may also want to talk about what rituals we could create that would strengthen and celebrate our bonds as a community.

To prepare for a community potluck, think about what food you might bring and what experiences you might contribute:

### DISCUSSION

Think about Putnam's thesis and the evolution of your family. Think about your communities of faith, gender, ethnicity, geography, education, and interests. How does your experience of community compare with that of your parents or grandparents? Would you say that you have a greater or lesser experience of community? How were their communities different from yours? What are some of the benefits of being connected with others? In what ways have you been supported and encouraged by these communities?

*Foods that I might contribute to a cultural potluck:*

*Memories of the family dinner table as I was growing up:*

*My experiences in visiting other cultures and communities:*

*Ideas for creating dinner rituals with friends and family:*

*We all should know that diversity makes for a rich tapestry, and we must understand that all the threads of the tapestry are equal in value no matter what their color.*

MAYA ANGELOU

*Ideas for creating rituals for our learning community:*

## COMMUNITY MAPPING: CORRELATING COMMUNITY AND HAPPINESS

Create a map of the communities you're involved in, noting the values of each community. Since these communities evolve around you, write your name in a circle in the middle of a page. Draw an arrow out from the circle. At the end of the arrow draw another circle representing a community you belong to. Write the name of the community inside the circle. Create as many arrows and circles as there are communities. On a scale of 1–10, with 10 being the highest, how involved are you in each community? Write the number inside each circle. Tally up your total and divide by the number of communities to find your community involvement index. Now, think about Robert Putnam's thesis about happiness. How happy are you? Does your happiness correlate with your level of community involvement?

# the nature of
# service

*Objective: Understand the purpose and experience of service.*

**EXCERPTS FROM ENGAGING THE NEXT GENERATION**

**VOLUNTEERING VS. VOTING**

**IN THE SERVICE OF LIFE**

**RANDOM ACTS OF SERVICE**

**START SMALL**

**STARTING SMALL**

**INTERVIEWING A COMMUNITY LEADER OR VOLUNTEER**

**FINDING INSPIRATION IN THE MEDIA**

## unit two

## THE NATURE OF SERVICE

*Objective: Understand the purpose and experience of service.*

*We make a living by what we get. We make a life by what we give.*

WINSTON CHURCHILL

In preparing for service, we need to explore the meaning of service, our motives for serving, and our expectations. What is service? How do we know when we have been served? How will we know when we have served others? What does it take for service to deepen our connections with one another? Can service be short, spontaneous, high-speed? Can it be deep, enriching, and mutual?

It's important to remember that as we serve others, we also benefit. Our service may be reciprocated directly with favors, appreciation, and love, or more indirectly with friendlier neighbors, a safer community, and more enlightened social policies. Service expands our awareness, awakens our empathy, deepens our relationships, and strengthens our hearts. It builds the bonds of community and our trust in one another. As you serve, ask yourself, "What am I receiving?"

What can we learn about the possibilities and challenges from others who have served? Reading, hearing and seeing stories about people who have served can inspire us to expand our ideas of service and to continue to share the light as they have done.

highlights and excerpts from

# Engaging the Next Generation:
## How Nonprofits Can Reach Young Adults

There are currently 27 million young people between the ages of 18-24 in the United States, a whopping 13% of the adult population. They have grown up with their own unique sensibilities, with more ethnically diverse peers, and in a world that is changing dramatically each moment. A list compiled by the faculty at Beloit College in Wisconsin demonstrates how drastically different their worldview is from that of older Americans. They were born into a world without Atari or record albums. Most have never seen a TV set that stops at channel 13. They do not remember the Cold War and have no fear of nuclear war.

### Who are these young people?

- 66% of 1998 high school graduates went on to college, up from 62% in 1992.

- Young adults today are individualistic, media savvy, and extremely stressed out.

- Young adults view "community" in a variety of ways—as their neighborhoods, the people they know, their religious institutions, their schools, their work, and their families.

### How many of them are currently volunteering?

- Of the 27 million 18-24 year olds in the U.S., 46% said they had volunteered in the past year (from the Independent Sector's publication, *Giving and Volunteering in the United States*, 1998). Some 29% of them volunteered in the past month, and they volunteered an average of three hours per week.

- Today's young people have no clear common causes to rally around, and so are much more likely to take their own unique approaches to getting involved.

a publication of the Advertising Council and MTV, which is available on-line at www.adcouncil.org

- Young adults are open to finding several different ways to care, as opposed to previous generations who often wanted to find one specific cause to believe in.

- In 1998 less than half (43%) of 18-24 year olds were asked to volunteer. Of that group, 87% volunteered (from the Independent Sector's publication, *Giving and Volunteering in the United States*, 1998). Of the 57% who weren't asked, only 16% volunteered.

### Generation X versus Generation Y

This audience of 18-24 year olds straddles both Generation X and Generation Y. It is important to distinguish between the two groups. Gen X'ers are held by demographic experts to be those born between 1965-1980, meaning they are currently ages 22-37. Today's 18 and 19 year olds are the beginning of Generation Y, a group known as the Echo Boom or Baby Boomlet generation. Generation X'ers are generally considered to be fiercely independent—they only trust in themselves, largely because so many of them are the product of divorce —realistic, pessimistic (they graduated into a recession), savvy, skeptical of marketing, and looking to create their own definitions of success. Generation Y is similar, but much more optimistic, more social and group-oriented, more empowered because of their computer and Web expertise, and entrepreneurial—13 year olds talk of growing up to be entrepreneurs.

## VOLUNTEERING VS. VOTING

A study conducted in June 1999 by the League of Women Voters indicated that just over half (51%) of young people ages 18-30 want to become more involved in community and volunteer activities. To put that statistic in context, roughly a third indicated that they do at least occasional volunteer work. Compare that to census figures showing that in 1996 only 32% of 18-24 year olds voted, as a decline in young voting continued—a decline that started in 1972, when the voting age was lowered to 18. The bottom line is that young adults told us that they do care about issues, and they want to be involved. They simply want to express themselves and get involved in their own way.

It is partially this reasoning that leads young people to be much more engaged in volunteering than they are in voting. In volunteer activities, young people say they can witness the changes they are making and the effects they are having on people's lives. Voting, on the other hand, is often seen as not making a difference to anyone except for the politician who is trying to advance his or her career. As a result of this cynicism, 18-24 year olds pay much less attention to national and local politics. According to Project Vote Smart, only 26% of 18-24 year olds say they pay a lot of attention to national politics, as compared to 45% of those over the age of 26.

**DISCUSSION**

How do you feel about these research findings? Do they confirm what you know about yourself and your peers? How does your experience with volunteering compare with the national statistics? Did someone ask you to volunteer or was it required for a class? Does the profile of young adults seem to fit you and the people you know? Do you vote? How do you account for the decline in voting and the decline in the number of young people who pay attention to national politics? What implications does that have for our society?

**JOURNALING**

What does service mean to you? Spend time journaling about your best experiences of serving others and reflect on why the experiences were meaningful for you. In journaling about service, consider the following questions: Do you have a parent who volunteers? Have you been involved in volunteer activity through a youth group, a religious organization, or a school? How have you benefited from serving others?

# In the Service of Life

by Rachel Naomi Remen

*Adele Gaboury, seventy-three, had great neighbors. They took care of her lawn, looked after her mail, and tended to broken pipes. They missed one item: she was dead, four years dead, in a pile of trash on her kitchen floor. The Worcester, Massachusetts woman was a noted recluse. Her brother made inquiries in 1989, but after locating a woman with the same last name in a nursing home, he assumed it was her.*

FROM THE *PRESS DEMOCRAT* TOP NEW STORIES OF 1992

In recent years the question *how can I help?* has become meaningful to many people. But perhaps there is a deeper question we might consider. Perhaps the real question is not *how can I help?* but *how can I serve?*

Serving is different from helping. Helping is based on inequality; it is not a relationship between equals. When you help you use your own strength to help those of lesser strength. If I'm attentive to what's going on inside of me when I'm helping, I find that I'm always helping someone who's not as strong as I am, who is needier than I am. People feel this inequality. When we help we may inadvertently take away from people more than we could ever give them; we may diminish their self-esteem, their sense of worth, integrity and wholeness. When I help I am very aware of my own strength. But we don't serve with our strength, we serve with ourselves. We draw from all of our experiences. Our limitations serve, our wounds serve, even our darkness can serve. The wholeness in us serves the wholeness in others and the wholeness in life. The wholeness in you is the same as the wholeness in me. Service is a relationship between equals.

Helping incurs debt. When you help someone they owe you one. But serving, like healing, is mutual. There is no debt. I am as served as the person I am serving. When I help I have a feeling of satisfaction. When I serve I have a feeling of gratitude. These are very different things.

Serving is also different from fixing. When I fix a person I perceive them as broken, and their brokenness requires me to act. When I fix I do not see the wholeness in the other person or trust the integrity or the life in them. When I serve I see and trust that wholeness. It is what I am responding to and collaborating with.

There is a distance between ourselves and whatever or whomever we are fixing. Fixing is a form of judgment. All judgment creates distance, a disconnection, an experience of difference. In fixing there is an inequality of expertise that can easily become a moral distance. We cannot serve at a distance. We can only serve that to which we are profoundly connected, that which we are willing to touch. This is Mother Teresa's basic message. We serve life not because it is broken but because it is holy.

If helping is an experience of strength, fixing is an experience of mastery and expertise. Service, on the other hand, is an experience of mystery, surrender and awe. A fixer has the illusion of being casual. A server knows that he or she is being used and has a willingness to be used in the service of something greater, something essentially unknown. Fixing and helping are very personal; they are very particular, concrete and specific. We fix and help many different things in our lifetimes, but when we serve we are always serving the same thing. Everyone who has ever served through the history of time serves the same thing. We are servers of the wholeness and mystery in life.

The bottom line, of course, is that we can fix without serving. And we can help without serving. And we can serve without fixing or helping. I think I would go so far as to say that fixing and helping may often be the work of the ego, and service the work of the soul. They may look similar if you're watching from the outside, but the inner experience is different. The outcome is often different, too.

Our service serves us as well as others. That which uses us strengthens us. Over time, fixing and helping are draining, depleting. Over time we burn out. Service is renewing. When we serve, our work itself will sustain us.

Service rests on the basic premise that the nature of life is sacred, that life is a holy mystery which has an unknown purpose. When we serve, we know that we belong to life and to that purpose. Fundamentally, helping, fixing and service are ways of seeing life. When you help you see life as weak; when you fix, you see life as broken. When you serve, you see life as whole. From the perspective of service, we are all connected: All suffering is like my suffering and all joy is like my joy. The impulse to serve emerges naturally and inevitably from this way of seeing.

Lastly, fixing and helping are the basis of curing, but not of healing. In 40 years of chronic illness I have been helped by many people and fixed by a great many others who did not recognize my wholeness. All that fixing and helping left me wounded in some important and fundamental ways. Only service heals.

**RANDOM ACTS OF SERVICE**

Consider this: What really is service? Are there other ways to serve beyond the ways we already know, beyond volunteering at local shelters, beyond the kind of service projects you might have been forced to do in the past?

Break up into small groups of three or four. Take five minutes to come up with a quick plan for offering and observing random acts of service. Who might benefit from what you as a group have to offer? How would you like to be served? What small act might make a big difference in your own life? Think for a moment. Use what you have, what you're good at, your art, your sense of humor, your compassion. Use whatever you can to celebrate the human part of somebody.

Now it's time to leave your learning community to look for and perform acts of service. Be as creative as possible and be ready to improvise, to discover, and to rethink as you go. Take forty-five minutes and keep a list to present to the class when you return. How easy was it to serve, to find people in need of service? Was it enjoyable? Was there a sense of play, invention, fun? Was it expensive to serve, did it cost a lot in effort or time? Did you experience or observe the distinction between serving, fixing, and helping?

In the end, we see that service has much more to do with our own awareness and our own intentions than the consequences of the act. Perhaps the result of your service was only a smile, or a laugh, or a thank-you. What is the resulting consequence of that gesture, however small, simple? What would be the ideal effect if everyone carried the awareness of service around with them? What does it mean then to serve?

**?**

*How would you distinguish between serving, fixing, and helping?*

*What metaphors does Remen use for each?*

*When have you been served? How did it feel?*

*When have you been fixed/helped? How did it feel?*

*Is it ever appropriate to help or fix?*

One argument against serving is that we can never do enough to make a real difference. This is Ram Dass' argument for "starting small."

# start small

In recent years in North America it has been hard to escape painful social realities such as hunger, homelessness, illiteracy, and drug abuse. If all we read is the daily newspaper, we still learn more than we have ever before known about the complex and long-lasting causes of poverty and prejudice. It has become easy to feel overwhelmed by the enormity of the suffering and apathetic about the possibility of change. Derek Bok, as president of Harvard, wrote that "there is disturbing evidence to suggest that most forms of responsibility towards others have eroded in recent decades." And Charles M. Vest, president of Massachusetts Institute of Technology, said recently, "As I look around the nation, I do fear that we are throwing up our hands in the face of very difficult social and educational issues."

It can certainly look that grim. And as long as we see suffering as an "issue" or a monolithic social problem, such as homelessness, hunger, or AIDS, we will find it difficult to act. The enormity of the suffering leaves us feeling dwarfed and powerless. And even a single person's pain may seem too big if we think of taking it on by ourselves.

Yet each of us can do something. Walking three miles to work won't heal the whole ozone layer, but it is something one person can do. And although we each can't do everything, together we can make a difference. Each of these bignesses is made up of many small parts. Individual people, sometimes working in groups. Individual moments. It is like the AIDS quilt, stitched together by the NAMES Project. Each patch is small, personal, and handmade. Each one reflects the person who made it and his or her friend, lover, or child who died of AIDS. Each patch is different: sweet, sophisticated, loving, stylish, outrageous. Together they make an immense blanket of love, care, sadness, and beauty. Like the Vietnam Veterans Memorial in Washington D.C., which lists the names of all the Americans who died in that confusing war, it is difficult to see the quilt without feeling simultaneously the poignancy of each individual patch and the power of the entire statement.

Each small act is part of a great fabric. The AIDS quilt doesn't replace the need for government responsibility—it points to it. And it is interesting that the big problems are exactly the ones that may find their solutions in small, creative, offbeat, unlikely ideas.

by Ram Dass

**STARTING SMALL**

Think about someone you know, a friend or a family member, who could use support. What do they need right now that you could provide? Perhaps you could help cook dinner, do the dishes, run an errand, install a computer program, proofread an important paper, play their favorite game, or listen to their stories. Offer an act of service. Describe the experience in a one-page paper and explain why it felt like serving and not helping or fixing. How does it feel to offer service to someone that you know? What impact does it have on your relationship? Be aware of other acts of service that you give and receive during the week and what it feels like to be served, fixed, or helped.

New to Chicago, Bill McBride had just heard that his college roommate had AIDS. One night in a neighborhood bar, he was handed a pamphlet describing a residence for people with AIDS. "We need help," the person who handed him the pamphlet said. "Will you help?" Surprised at himself, Bill agreed immediately.

With a friend for moral support, Bill arrived at Chicago House, a large home in the uptown section of the city. The director asked him what he could do. "Well," Bill said, "I am an editor and a teacher, so I guess I could read to people. "They don't want that," the director answered, but Bill persevered. "Well, I can cook—I grew up in the South—my mother taught me." " That might be good," the director said, "but don't come with any expectations. Maybe no one will eat the food." Apprehensive but willing to try, Bill returned a few nights later by subway with one of his favorite dishes. To his delight, it was a hit; it led to him being called Casserole Queen. And it came from a simple beginning, following the basic guidelines: be brave, start small, use what you've got, do something you enjoy, don't overcommit.

Later, as Bill began to appreciate the many problems associated with helping people with AIDS and to realize the need in the AIDS community for greater financial support, he wanted to do more. Working as an editor during the day and cooking at night, Bill, with the help of his friend Jim LiSacchi, thought of creating and marketing a cookbook that would benefit people with AIDS. Calling on help from some of Chicago's greatest chefs, they created *Specialties of the House: Great Recipes from Great Chicago Restaurants*. The dedication page reads: "To lend a helping hand in a time of need is to strengthen the spirit and compassion of all humanity." The book sold well, raised money for Chicago House, and became a model for similar projects in other cities.

There are opportunities everywhere. They may present themselves even when we stop at a neighborhood bar. A hospice worker adjusts a patient's pillow, a cabdriver at the end of her shift drives a pregnant woman to the hospital, a shelter "family" stands in a circle of silence before their meal, a development worker in Mexico keeps extra blankets in her apartment for visiting refugees. The small things carry a message of caring. They say that each one of us matters.

Amnesty International recruits volunteers to write letters to prisoners of conscience. It seems like a small thing to do. A Moroccan prisoner wrote back: "For us the letter is the outside, the forbidden! It increases the hope to see, some day in the future, unknown strands, the world of our imperfect dreams, the world of the living."

High school senior Asha Nadkarni volunteered to visit mentally retarded adults in a state school on their birthdays. She would take each patient a cupcake and a balloon. She reported, "Meeting these people was discovering a purity found in most children and envied by most adults.... Perhaps the touch of someone young brightened their day. Maybe they went to bed that night a little happier than the night before. It was a little thing I did; it's hard to save the world with a cupcake. But who couldn't use a birthday party?"

Small is, in fact, beautiful. Human-scale undertakings based on common sense are the most likely to succeed. As E. F. Schumacher said, "Small scale operations...are always less likely to be harmful than large scale ones. There is wisdom in smallness even if only on account of the smallness and patchiness of human knowledge."

When Joanne Eccher and friends started the Hunger Hotline in Boston, their ambitious goals were to "get different legislation passed and do advocacy work with food pantries and soup kitchens and do litigation work to raise welfare benefits and get food stamps expanded." But when they met with the people in the community, they found that "the first thing they wanted was rats and roaches out of their pantries. And the next thing they wanted was better food at their meals. And then vans and transportation. And I remember thinking, Vans and transportation. We're just contributing to the charitable aspect. But after some time we realized that people's basic human needs had to be met and trust had to be established before they could begin to ask why they were in such a situation. We had to start with the small things before we could deal with the bigger issues."

When a project starts with a minimal investment and just a few people, there is little to lose; the project can take more risks, play closer to the edge, and reveal new ways of dealing with intractable problems. Such solutions can then be a model for others. Or the "multiplier effect" may occur, in which those people who learn in a small project teach others how to do something in their communities, and those people then teach more people.

During their Harvard Law School summers, Alan Khazei and Michael Brown had both worked in Washington for lawmakers trying to create a federally financed national youth service corps, a kind of domestic Peace Corps. Their dream was of teenagers across the country giving a year of their lives to providing new life to America's cities while learning about teamwork, caring for others, the richness of social diversity, and the great feeling that comes from making a difference after you've worked hard. As the proposals lingered in congressional committees, they began to realize that there might be too many obstacles to starting with a government-sponsored, national plan, especially with a Republican administration governing a skeptical population. But they were still close enough to their own adolescence to remember its incredible energy looking for expression.

They returned to Boston and, after an experimental summer program, recruited fifty young people, seventeen to twenty-two years old. It was a racially, ethnically, economically, and socially diverse group—rich, poor, black, white, Latino, Asian, suburban preppy, inner-city gang—to "walk with, and help out, Boston's most vulnerable residents: the poor, the homeless, and the mentally and physically disabled." With money from foundations and corporations, City Year gives each of its members a stipend of $100 a week and a $5,000 college scholarship at the end of a year of service. The corps has started and now manages an after-school program for children at a low-income housing development. It has salvaged and distributed 130 tons of surplus food, painted a shelter for the homeless, and repaired and cleaned the homes of senior citizens in East Boston. In a ghetto storefront, the City Year team has tutored scores of Latino youths in reading and math and served as role models for them. It has carried out a census of the homeless, worked in nursing homes, and cleaned up a tot lot. Equally satisfying to Mike Brown, however, are the changes in the corps members themselves, whom he sees as developing the qualities of "involved citizenry," which he feels needs to be restored in our democracy if it is going to survive.

When we act, we can see our feelings of powerlessness dissolve. Movements such as the antiwar movement, the civil rights movement, and the labor movement began with individual acts by caring human beings such as Rosa Parks, who simply sat in the front of the bus, and Ron Kovic, who spoke out for veterans by speaking out for himself. At their most effective these movements were still simply the total of all those individual people acting to bring the changes they believed in. And, as some folks say, if Rosa Parks hadn't sat down, Martin Luther King, Jr., would never have stood up.

When we start small, we are more likely to remember that not only is it okay to be ourselves but in fact that is the most important thing. We can't be Martin Luther King, Jr., or Rosa Parks. We can be inspired by them, but even if we try we can't be them. We have to be ourselves. As ancient wisdom tells us, "Do not seek to follow in the footsteps of the men (or women) of old; seek what they sought." We have to look and see what *we* can do.

Tutoring can be a help. Childcare can be a help. Casseroles can be a help. There were many happy meals at Chicago House, during which people dying of AIDS told one another their stories and laughed about some of the absurdities of life. Maybe your style is brandied chicken with green peppercorns or hot apple cake with caramel pecan sauce. Give it a try. Start small, and give yourself a chance to find out. Begin alone, or begin with others, but keep it simple. And remember the words of Margaret Mead, who said, "Never doubt that a small group of thoughtful, committed citizens can change the world; indeed it's the only thing that ever has."

*Of all the stories about service in this essay, which one is most inspiring for you?*

*What are some of the advantages of starting small?*

*What are some qualities of an informed citizen? How would you describe the ideal citizen?*

*When have you offered a small service to another person? What was the response? How did it make you feel?*

# INTERVIEWING A COMMUNITY LEADER OR VOLUNTEER

Before you take action on a service project, think about what you might encounter. What are your fears or concerns? What do you need to consider or prepare to be sure that your service is meaningful for you and helpful to others?

One useful way to prepare for service is to talk with a community leader, a volunteer, or a representative from a nonprofit organization. This person will be able to help you plan for your service experience and prepare for the new people and ideas that you may encounter. Meet with a nonprofit or community leader, someone with service experience, to talk about his/her experiences with service, what can be learned, what are the challenges. What can/should you expect? How can you meet and serve others in a way that is mutually respectful? You might also be able to learn about career opportunities in the public interest or nonprofit sector.

Here are some questions you may want to ask:

*How did you begin volunteering?*

*What motivated you to serve?*

*What rewards have you received from serving?*

*What challenges have you faced?*

*What advice would you give to others who want to begin serving?*

## FINDING INSPIRATION IN THE MEDIA

Reading, meeting, seeing, and hearing about others who serve can give us ideas about our own service opportunities. These two following exercises can help students deepen their understanding of service and begin to contemplate the possibilities for service in their own lives.

To increase your understanding of service, look for stories about people who serve in books and newspapers, radio, TV, film, and on the Internet. You may find inspiring stories about community volunteers in your neighborhood newspaper. You may also be inspired by listening to *The Cellist of Sarajevo*, an interview from *All Things Considered* that is available on the National Public Radio Website, by watching a documentary such as *Scout's Honor* by Tom Shepard, which ran on PBS's P.O.V. series and which tells the story of one boy's mission to change the policy of the Boy Scouts so that the organization is inclusive of all boys no matter what their sexual identity, or even by enjoying commercial films such as *Groundhog Day* and *Pay It Forward*, which have strong messages about the value of service in giving meaning to life.

# unit three
# opportunities
## to serve

*Objective: Consider interests and skills in the process of identifying opportunities to serve.*

**CONSIDER YOUR OPTIONS**

**THE SERVICE LOTTERY**

**IDENTIFY YOUR INTERESTS**

**IDENTIFY YOUR TALENTS AND RESOURCES**

**RESEARCH YOUR OPTIONS**

**PUT IT ALL TOGETHER**

## OPPORTUNITIES TO SERVE

*Objective: Consider interests and skills in the process of identifying opportunities to serve.*

*Never doubt that a small group of thoughtful, committed people can change the world. Indeed, it is the only thing that ever has.*

MARGARET MEAD

**S**elf-reflection is the key to identifying the service opportunities that will be of the greatest benefit to you and to the people and causes that you choose to serve. What problems have affected your life or the lives of people who are important to you? When you read the newspaper or watch the news, which people and which problems catch your eye and touch your heart?

Where would you like to make a difference? What skills and resources can you offer, and where can they make the most impact? Here are a few exercises to help you identify your calling to serve.

**CONSIDER YOUR OPTIONS**

Here is a list of possibilities for you to consider. Circle the issues that are most compelling for you, where you feel that you might make a difference:

## Arts

Outreach to New Populations and Areas

Arts Education and Appreciation for Children and Youth

Arts Funding and Policy Issues

Freedom of Expression

Arts for Social Change

Other:

## Education

School Reform

Character Education

Literacy

Media Literacy

Child Care

Violence Prevention

Other:

## Social Service and Special Populations

Blind and Visually Impaired

Deaf and Hearing Impaired

Mental Health Treatment and Advocacy

Child Abuse Prevention

Veterans' Support

Elderly/Aging

Housing/Homeless

Feeding the Hungry

Other:

## Health

Cancer Cure/Prevention

AIDS Cure/Prevention

Health Insurance and Health Care Reform

Crisis Intervention

Social Security

Medicare

Other:

# Environment

Littering

Recycling

Pollution

Urban Renewal

Mass Transit

Global Warming/Greenhouse Effect

Preservation of Nature/Waterways

Alternative Energy Sources

Water and Energy Conservation

Nuclear Waste Disposal

Environmental Justice

Other:

# Global and Local Community Issues

Poverty/Growing Gap between Rich and Poor

Immigration/Refugee Issues

Legal and Welfare Rights/Civil Rights/Racism

Criminal Justice/Death Penalty/International Criminal Court

Voter Registration

Campaign Finance Reform

Corporate Responsibility and Accountability

Concentration of Ownership in the Media

Political Activism

Taxes/Government Spending

Human Rights

Ecumenical Movements

Peace and Understanding

Other:

# Other Options

**THE SERVICE LOTTERY**

Imagine that you have won a very special lottery in which all of your living expenses will be covered for the next five years. You are asked to use your talents and skills along with $100,000 each year to do whatever will most benefit the community or serve humanity. Use your journal to list all of the people and issues you might want to serve and the projects you might want to undertake when you win this "service lottery."

Now, even without these resources, how might you start on one of these projects?

**IDENTIFY YOUR INTERESTS**

Look back at your community map and think about each community. What does each community need? What would most help that community? Next to each community, make some notes about services you might provide or projects that you might initiate.

Then think about the situation or need in the world that most touches your heart. With whose hopes do you identify? With whose suffering do you sympathize? Whose rights would you choose to defend? What wrongs need to be addressed?

**IDENTIFY YOUR TALENTS & RESOURCES**

Circle all of the talents, skills, and resources that you have and that you have access to:

Drawing

Writing

Producing

Acting

Dancing

Singing

Designing

Painting

Decorating

Organizing

Planning

Promoting

Appreciating

Teaching

Shooting video

Taking photographs

Arranging exhibits

Writing music

Playing an instrument

Searching the Internet

Creating Web pages

Cooking

Building

Space

Equipment

Supplies

Computers

Funds

Transportation

Contacts

Other:

## RESEARCH YOUR OPTIONS

# Now it's time to research your options.

You can go on-line and use a search engine to gather information about a cause, issue, or organization. You may also want to search the Internet for ideas about how, when, and where to do service.

Here are some examples of past Senior Seminar group service projects:

# The Butterfly Game

Students organized a morning of fun for children at a local day care center, writing a song about butterflies, helping children make and wear their butterfly headbands, and leading the children in the butterfly dance and other games.

# Greater Chicago Food Depository

This class packed, unpacked, sorted, and stacked food that had been donated to the food depository.

# Pacific Garden Mission

The students worked with homeless people to create a radio show and to improve the radio station at the mission.

# Croatia Children's Relief Packet

The students created audiotapes of children's stories with accompanying hand puppets. The materials were sent to Zagreb, Croatia, to a refugee camp of more than 250,000 people.

# Seniors to Seniors

The students interviewed residents of a nursing home to find out about their needs and interests. The residents said that they wanted to get out of the home to walk to the lake or shop at a neighborhood store, so the students arrived one afternoon to host a party and take them out for walks and errands.

# Visiting a Pet Shelter

The students spent hours walking and playing with unwanted dogs and cats.

## Thurgood Marshall Middle School

Working with eighty students at this school, seniors created a documentary about their reading and understanding of *To Kill a Mockingbird*.

## Holiday Service

These students adopted a single mom and her three children for Christmas, using class funds to buy a $100 gift certificate for clothes and shoes and three age-appropriate presents for the children. Another class decorated a preschool for the holidays.

## Clothing Drive

This class collected warm clothing and made lunches to give to people living on the streets.

## Stories from Seniors

These students visited a nursing home to collect stories from the residents and make them into a book that was given to the home as a memento.

## Art Festival Benefit

The students produced a winter arts festival, organizing an exhibition and performances, lining up the venue, and creating and distributing the marketing materials. All proceeds were donated to charity.

## Cookout for Freshmen

The seniors organized a cookout, invited freshmen to be their guests, and gave the freshmen advice about how to succeed in college.

## Children's Crafts at the Zoo

This class set up a booth at the Lincoln Park Zoo to do crafts projects with children.

*The more you try to be interested in other people, the more you find out about yourself.*

THEA ASTLEY

**PUT IT ALL TOGETHER**

Look back at your answers to the "Service Lottery" exercise and at the items you've circled on the lists of issues and talents. Where might they overlap? What community service ideas come to mind? List them here:

1)

2)

3)

serving

# together

## and learning from service

## unit four

*Objective: Plan and implement a group community service project and reflect on its impact.*

## SERVING TOGETHER AND LEARNING FROM SERVICE

*Objective: Plan and implement a group community service project and reflect on its impact.*

*The human contribution is the essential ingredient. It is only in the giving of oneself to others that we truly live.*

ETHEL PERCY ANDRUS

While many students may have personal experiences with service, this may be the first time that they work together with a group and with each other to plan a group project. In this unit, the students will do a team-building exercise to identify any strengths and challenges that need to be addressed in their project planning and implementation. The students can work together to plan and implement their project, using the suggestions and checklist provided in this unit. Both the experience and reflection about the experience may be enhanced if students can document their planning, preparation, decision making, and service. Perhaps some students will serve the team by documenting the process with photographs, videos, stories, oral histories, or a Website.

**COMPASS POINTS**

This exercise, originally developed by members of the National School Reform Faculty, helps team members identify their individual styles of working within a group and helps them recognize the value of all styles when working toward a common team goal or product. Think about your own experience of working in a group. Which of these descriptions best fits you?

North: Acting—"Let's do it!" Likes to act, try things, plunges in.

East: Speculating—Likes to look at the big picture, the possibilities, before acting.

South: Caring—Likes to know that everyone's feelings have been taken into consideration, that their voices have been heard before acting.

West: Paying Attention to Detail—Likes to know the who, what, when, where, why, before acting.

If these are four basic ways to participate in teamwork, what do they mean for planning and implementing a project together? What would be the best combination for a group to have? Does it matter? How can you avoid being driven crazy by another "direction"? How can you fully employ your strengths as a group and compensate for any areas where you might be weak?

## BUILDING A TEAM AND APPRECIATING DIFFERENCES

Before we begin working together on a group service project, it's important to study, experience, and celebrate community because it is through and with communities that we become most fully ourselves and where we find the most compelling and challenging opportunities to serve. By working together in communities and in groups, we learn about our similarities and our differences. We learn to appreciate the strengths that others bring and the potential and the challenges of diversity. We also develop the ability to look at our group behavior and to develop an understanding about the strengths and weaknesses of our communal efforts.

## HOW TO CHOOSE A GROUP PROJECT

By Kris Larsen

You can use a fishbowl exercise to choose a group service project. Separate into two groups and ask the first group to sit in a circle and ask the other group to sit around them on the outside to act as observers. Ask the group to brainstorm on possible communities that they have served or could serve and record their suggestions in a visible location. While this process goes on, the outside group listens and offers feedback as to any obstacles that they may sense as to the decision of communities to serve, pointing out, for example, when the brainstorming group becomes defocused on the task. When the first group has created a list of all possible communities, the groups change places and the process begins anew. At the end of this process there will be a large number of communities on the list and as you go down the list, the group can then say yea or nay about serving each community. Or, an alternative way to narrow down the list would be to give each person four dots to vote for the communities that most interest them. Once the list of potential communities has been narrowed down to two or three, the class can then gather more information, continue brainstorming to develop plans and options, and then determine the best opportunity based on interests, timing, and availability.

# COMMUNITY SERVICE PREPARATION CHECKLIST

Prepare for the service project by visiting the site and interviewing participants to determine their needs. This is an opportunity to discuss what everyone hopes to achieve and what everyone can contribute to the experience. The class might want to send a few representatives to make the initial contact and to develop a list of priorities and protocols. "The Community Service Preparation Checklist," which was used to plan a visit to a day care center, can serve as a template for the questions and activities associated with the service project.

*If every American donated five hours a week, it would equal the labor of 20 million full-time volunteers.*

WHOOPI GOLDBERG

## Day Care Center Visit Checklist

*Goals for Senior Seminar Students:*

*Goals for the Children:*

*Names, locations, and phone numbers for contact people:*

*Planning Meeting: Date, Location, Participants, Agenda*

*Service Experience: Date, Location, Participants, Timetable*

*Materials: What will we need? What will the children need? Who is responsible?*

*Setup: What needs to be produced or organized before the visit? Before the children and families arrive? Who is responsible?*

*Procedures and questions to be used in the activity (point-by-point guide for the activity). Who is responsible?*

*Cleanup: Who is responsible?*

*Documentation, Appreciation, and Closure: Who is responsible?*

*Other Considerations/Additional Information:*

## Discussion

Questions to consider about the community service project: Is this community one that the group is comfortable working with? What do we need to know about the organization or community before we go in? What should the organization or community know about the students before they arrive? How can we best listen to the needs of this community or organization?

## REFLECTING ON OUR SERVICE EXPERIENCE

In reflection we harvest the benefits of our experience. To receive the full benefit of the service experience, you will write about the experience in your journal and debrief the experience in class using a protocol such as "What, So What, Now What?" Each of you will also write a paper describing the service experience. You will read your papers in class to deepen your sense of community with one another and to learn from each other's experiences.

Here are two ways to reflect on your experience:

According to Kolb's theory, one must go through four phases to learn from an experience. Using these four components, write about your service project experience:

Concrete Experience: The facts about your experience.

Reflection: Personal thoughts about that experience.

Conceptualization: A review of past learning or reading that might relate to that experience.

Experimentation: A generalization or "lesson drawn" from the experience. What did you learn about organization and team building? About service? About yourself?

•

Tell a story about the community service project, including the following:

A discussion of the overall vision/mission of the project

An evaluation of the group process in organizing the project, including your role in the group planning and your typical way of functioning in groups

A description of the event itself (who, what, when, where, and how)

Your evaluation of the effectiveness of the project

Your personal involvement in the actual project

Your thoughts on the nature of service and its relation to a successful life

## EXCERPTS FROM COMMUNITY SERVICE PAPERS
## BY STUDENTS IN THE SENIOR SEMINAR

"Let's play tiger hunt." As I said the words I knew that I had set myself up for trouble. I knew that this would be a fun game but at the same time I didn't know if they would like it. That was one of the most satisfying moments that I had at Casa Central. The children loved it and we played it over twelve times. I remember when I was in kindergarten and I learned that game. It has been my favorite for as long as I can remember.

Service is a healer not only for people physically but also for their spirit. It's important because through serving people find a place where they matter to others and are loved; two things that we all crave. I know that I would not be who I am if I did not find so much pleasure in helping others; the good feeling that you get from helping your fellow man cannot be matched....

Megan Tanco
2002

I think the main thing that I learned is that everyone wants to be loved, and that everyone will do whatever is in their power to get it. I learned that giving helps not only the person who is receiving but it also helps you. In the words of Rachel Naomi Remen, "Our service serves us as well as others. That which uses us strengthens us." I know that what I went into Casa Central to do, I succeeded at. I came out with a new view of the world, I came out healed, and I came out with a mentality of service.

I can't lie. To say I had little enthusiasm for our classroom community service project would be an overstatement. I'm a senior, tired of school, tired of meaningless projects and tedious assignments, and tired of having to be in classes that felt more like a waste of time than of enlightenment. You could say I'm feeling just a tad bit jaded. This community service project was going to be just one more irritation. I remember wondering what the hell good we could really do a community in an almost embarrassingly short two-hour period. I mean seriously. My heart wasn't into it, I wasn't into it, and I didn't need to be there. As I began to identify the feelings I was experiencing it occurred to me: maybe I'm a little scared, too.

Sure I was upset at being forced to do something I didn't want to do, but moreover, I was just downright nervous. I really wasn't sure what we were getting into. I knew we were working with kids, however, and that worried me enough. I love kids but I'd never really been around them much less been forced to just spend time with twenty of them in the same room. What will I do? What will they do? Will it be really weird? These are questions I asked myself. I had no idea....

Joey Mapes
2000

I didn't know what to expect or what to do, but once I entered the classroom everything changed....When the kids saw me their eyes just lit up. Many of them wanted to know my name. Two of them began hugging me like I was their long lost father. At that point the uneasy feelings I had experienced left my body. There were no egos in this room, just a bunch of kids who needed attention and someone to play with. They were anxious to show me so many things: how to color in a star, how to make a cookie out of clay, and how to build a fortress out of paper blocks. Most of all, however, they showed me their innocence and how in need and deserving of love they all are.

●

Maria Santiago-Martinez
1999

I know that one day of volunteering my time to help the elderly isn't much. But I do know that those people appreciated what our classroom did for them. I could tell just by seeing the expression on their faces and hearing them singing and clapping their hands. Seeing their smiles and the expressions on their faces made a big difference for one day in their lives, and of course this one day too I will never forget because I know that for that one moment in time I made someone happy and that happiness made my day too.

●

My class was throwing a Christmas party for the residents of the facility. It was our group community service project. We wanted to do some type of service for the elderly. Our original choice was between children and the elderly. It seems that there are a lot of organizations that give support to children. However, the elderly are often sent away to places where strangers take care of them and the people they knew forget they exist.

When we walked into the room there were about ten people sitting quietly around tables. Most of them were in wheel chairs.... The guests looked at us from beneath their vacant stares. I was scared. They expected something from us. Of course they did. We were here to throw a party for them, spread some Christmas cheer. I did not know what to do. I am terrible at small talk.... I am like a turtle. I do not come out of my house until I know it is safe. It was not safe in that room. But I felt like it was my job to convince our guests that it was not only safe, but also comfortable. I was terrified.

Anuska Chorba
2000

At that point some more of my classmates had arrived. They were filling up a table with art supplies. I grabbed a handful of supplies from the table.... I went to three or four tables, doing card-making demonstrations.... I made a card with [one] woman. I gave her choices and she told me, "yes." Each time she said, "yes," I felt a little closer to her. She was smiling ear to ear. All my feelings of uneasiness evaporated. The room was still awful; but the party had started.

I cut and pasted and glued for my new friend. She seemed to enjoy watching me work and hearing me talk. She was just watching me and smiling.... I looked at the woman. Her hair was white. Her face was gray. But her smile was luminous. She did have a life and that life is still inside her, pulsing with the force of a thousand rivers. There was love in her life. And passion. And adventure. And heartbreak. And lust. And music. And dancing. And crying. And laughing. She was alive.... I realized that the secret in that room was that every one of those people was brimming with the experience and wisdom of a life.

The party turned out to be a success. It was wonderful despite my grim expectations. The reactions from the people were phenomenal. As we were leaving the party I wondered if I would remember that day when I was older. I wondered if I would remember it next year. If I would be able to see the eyes of the man with cerebral palsy who led the room in a Christmas carol, or the people dancing in their wheel chairs when music filled the room. I am not sure. But the expression on that woman's face is inside me. I can see it right now, smiling and saying "yes."

In the selection of our group service project, my initial urge was to vote for a communal project that would provide the smallest amount of direct personal contact. I could build something or clean something or organize something or stuff envelopes. I just didn't want to interact with people, young or old, sick or healthy, in a big way. I don't dislike other people—so much. I just felt that one morning, a couple of hours, wouldn't make a huge difference in anybody's life.

Amanda Small
2000

Let's just say I walked into Casa Central with a hardened heart. "I'm not a 'kid' person," I told myself. We had our orientation, divided up into classrooms, and off we went to make a difference.

Thus began my morning with the preschoolers. A blow-by-blow account won't do this morning justice. Let me list some of the things that struck me:

- *The complete openness of the kids—no fear or distrust*
- *The ready hugs and throwing of young bodies against my legs*
- *The feel of their little warm hands in mine*
- *They were all bilingual! They'd switch easily from Spanish to English*
- *The adult personalities that were already forming*

It was an incredibly rewarding morning. The kids obviously enjoyed it, and the teachers really seemed to appreciate the help (although I think the volunteers were a bit soft when it came to classroom rules). And it made me really contemplate some choices I'd made. Mainly, the decision to not have children. They obviously move me. There's obviously a need for caring adults in so many arenas of kids' lives. Also, I had to address the selfishness —that's all I can call it—surrounding my attitude about this volunteer program. I obviously like the human contact, so why avoid it.

I guess this narrative is probably self-centered. How did I feel? What did I do? Why did the kids and their affection hit me so hard?

What I can say is that the experience really opened my eyes and destroyed some misconceptions about volunteering. Mainly, that it is a painful, boring experience. It's rewarding. Also, that you have to give hours and hours to really make a difference. A few hours make an impact. I made an impact. The children made an impact on me.

## DOCUMENTING THE SERVICE PROJECT

Here is an example of the strategy that a Senior Seminar class used to document their project. It's an article, describing the class community service project *Art for Young Hearts*, which appeared in the college newspaper, *Columbia College Chronicle*. As you plan your project, remember to recruit group members to document your service activities with a video, Website, flyer, or book. As examples, consider Joan Dickinson's book documenting the creation of a mosaic at a local elementary school and videos about the group community service projects at NEON Street and at the Thurgood Marshall School. It's also a good idea to submit a press release to your school newspaper and your local newspaper.

excerpt from
the *Columbia College Chronicle*

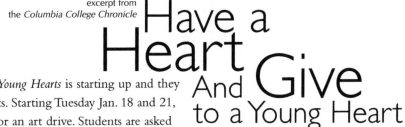

Have a Heart And Give to a Young Heart

A new organization called *Arts For Young Hearts* is starting up and they are looking for help from all students. Starting Tuesday Jan. 18 and 21, bins will be set up around campus for an art drive. Students are asked to donate any left-over or un-used art supplies such as markers, posterboard, pens, pencils, film, ink or whatever you can give. They are looking for donations of art supplies that will be given to first and third graders at Haines Middle School in Chinatown. Look for the *Arts For Young Hearts* logo on bins all around campus. President of *Arts For Young Hearts*, Mindy Geurink, suggested the idea for the new group and says children need people in the working world as well. "Not only do children need quality art supplies and experiences which we are working to collect and provide, they also need people to [show] that enormous satisfaction and incredible career opportunities can come from working within the arts."

Rose Economou is the group's advisor and helped start the grass roots organization and is hopeful that the group can make a difference in the lives of other students.

"They have established an identity in community and commitment to a progressive Chicago that includes arts and communications." The group even has their own Web site still under construction by Joe Rockey, one of the founding members, "I love it, I designed it, and I'm dedicated to this project."

The Web site can be accessed at *www.angelfire.com/il2/afhy/index.htm* which has more information about the organization, including ways to get involved and a history of how it started. The group has a mission statement that says: "As artists and ongoing supporters of the arts we strongly believe that music, drama, visual arts, and media arts deserve time, respect, and support in early childhood classrooms."

by Richard E. Ryzewki
*Columbia News and Notes*

# chapter 3

**DESIGNING VOCATION**

| | objective | outcome | readings | other elements |
|---|---|---|---|---|
| **unit 1** | Consider larger vocational issues than getting a job. | Students will explore the meaning and importance of vocation versus "job" for themselves. Students will be aware of rapid changes in the current work environment. Students will recognize what they want from their work environment. | Does Your Present Career Choice Fit? The Changing World of Work | Career Visualization Work Environments |
| **unit 2** | Understand and participate in a variety of networking opportunities. | Students will develop an appreciation for the art of networking. Students will experience a firsthand opportunity to practice networking skills. | New Ways to Network | Networking Tips How Do You Network? Informational Interviewing Business Card Tips Interview Someone In Your Field |
| **unit 3** | Prepare effective job search correspondence. | Students will develop skills to prepare a competitive resume and to produce job-specific cover letters and other job search correspondence. | Resumes Cover Letters Thank-You Letters | Accomplishments Inventory |
| **unit 4** | Explore job search strategies and prepare for successful, professional interviews. | Students will become aware of strategies for job searching other than newspaper ads and Websites. Students will gain knowledge and practice that will help them to participate in successful interviewing. | Finding Job Openings and Opportunities The Basics of Job Searching Go Roundabout How to Submit Your Stuff Extra Stuff Marching to a Different Drummer Tips for Managing Your Job Search Say Good-Bye to Chicago Other Tips The Inside Track to Creative Jobs Interviewing Tips | Are You Ready for Your Job Search? Recommended Reading Interview Journal |

---

**DESIGNING VOCATION**

*If you do not feel yourself growing in your work and your life broadening and deepening, if your task is not a perpetual tonic to you, you have not found your place.*

ORISON SWETT MARDEN

Now it is time to double-check and make sure you are ready to go out and win that perfect professional position. (If you are already working happily in your chosen field, you may choose to use this chapter as a reference tool for the next time you find yourself in the job search process.)

You may be asking yourself at this point, "Have I really found the perfect career path—the work that will make me happy?" Since you will spend more time working than doing anything else, this is a very important question. Making the best possible career decision has enormous implications for the rest of your life. If you make the wrong decision, boredom or anxiety will follow you home from work and negatively impact other parts of your life. If you choose well, you will greet almost every morning with excitement and enthusiasm for the coming workday. Imagine spending your life doing something that you care about deeply, with the majority of your time engaged in activities that use your talents—your inherent greatness—naturally and fully.

So far, this book has helped you explore important questions about who you are, what's important to you, and how you can serve community. It's now time to apply what you have learned to career decisions. The idea of a perfect vocation is probably different for everyone, but Nicholas Lore has identified what he feels are the components of a perfect vocation. They include finding work that expresses all aspects of your temperament and personality, even those parts you do not see as positive; doing something in which you have a passionate and abiding interest; is challenging and requires you to learn and grow; is ecologically sound; and serves humanity in some way. And, of course, you must be able to make a living at it!

This perfect vocation, however, does not necessarily require lofty goals, such as saving the world or curing cancer. It does require finding a position where you can fully be yourself and where you have the feeling that you are doing the work because you choose to and not because you are compelled to do it. The work of a perfect vocation continually nourishes you and provides a natural path for your evolution.

This chapter, then, will help you find your perfect vocation or affirm that you have already found work that you love. It will also help you understand, obtain, and refine your job-searching skills and strategies, so you can actually find that perfect job.

First of all, it is crucial to understand the work world now as compared with the work world of the past. Why? Well, if you are a traditional-age college student (eighteen to twenty-five years of age), chances are your parents entered the work world in a much different environment than the current one. The strategies that worked in the past, such as pounding the pavement and sending out tons of resumes, are no longer applicable. What's more, in most fields it is no longer necessary to have completed a particular major that corresponds to a particular field. Many employers are willing to train individuals who are strong communicators, team players, and critical thinkers no matter what they majored in. What else has changed, and how quickly is it changing? What skills are employers looking for, now and in the future? These issues and more will be discussed.

Chances are the job you're looking for isn't going to be in the *Chicago Tribune* or the *New York Times*. It's also probably not on those fancy job search Websites. So, where to look? We will provide you with ideas and referrals. We will also discuss networking, one of the most important factors when searching for that perfect opportunity.

Searching for a job can feel like a full-time job in and of itself. It is important to start early and keep your spirits up. Looking for that perfect job takes time and a lot of energy. Of course, you also need the right tools. Through exercises and readings we will sort through the mysteries of resumes, cover letters, interviewing, and other job search correspondence. We will also suggest ways to organize it all.

## JOB SEARCH INVENTORY

Indicate which ones you've already accomplished:

___ I have joined a professional association in my field.

___ I have completed at least three informational interviews to discover where I want to work and narrow down job titles
I want to apply for.

___ I have volunteered in my profession or held at least one internship.

___ I have attended at least one professional workshop or conference outside of school.

___ I have made a list of the work-related values I will not compromise (e.g., health care benefits, a short commute,
continuing education, etc.)

___ I have prepared a list of my work-related skills for resume purposes.

___ I have researched the job market thoroughly and come up with several leads I am interested in.

___ I have prepared an organizer where I can keep track of job leads applied for, interviews held, and follow-up like
second interviews held and thank-you letters sent.

___ I have prepared a competitive resume and cover letter for each individual job lead.

___ I have met with my career advisor and faculty to review my resumes, cover letters, and supporting materials such
as portfolios, demo reels, headshots, etc.

___ I have kept an interview journal to prepare myself for interview questions.

___ I have developed a list of references.

# discovering
# vocation

## work that you love

**DOES YOUR PRESENT CAREER CHOICE FIT?**

**CAREER VISUALIZATION**

**THE CHANGING WORLD OF WORK**

**WORK ENVIRONMENTS**

## unit one

*Objective: Consider larger vocational issues than getting a job.*

# DISCOVERING VOCATION: WORK THAT YOU LOVE

*Objective: Consider larger vocational issues than getting a job.*

*Choose a job you love, and you will never have to work a day in your life.*

CONFUCIUS

n this unit, we will be exploring some of the larger issues surrounding career choice and the world of work. First, we will review your current career choice and make sure it is the best fit for you. Next, we will look at how the work world is changing and what you need to know about it to make good decisions. Finally, we will discuss personality style and how it relates to selecting your ideal work environment.

# DOES YOUR PRESENT CAREER CHOICE FIT?

Go over the following list. Use your current full-time or part-time job, or if you are not currently working, choose a job from the past. This will help you clarify your ideal work environment. Check the statements that are true. If you check almost all of them, you are doing pretty well. The ones you left unchecked show you where you could use some improvement. If you left several of them unchecked, you may need to explore some other options.

___ *You feel like a duck in a pond.*

___ *Your job fits you so well that, often, work is play.*

___ *You are proud of what you do and enjoy telling other people about it.*

___ *You are highly respected at work because you are so good at what you do.*

___ *You do not have to pretend to be someone else at work.*

___ *Your own best and most natural forms of creative expression are what you are paid to do.*

___ *The environment you work in brings out your best efforts.*

___ *You enthusiastically look forward to going to work most of the time.*

___ *Your job rewards your most important values and allows you to fulfill your goals in terms of personal growth, achievements, income, stability, etc.*

___ *The result of your efforts makes a contribution that personally matters to you. You don't spend your days working for something that you don't really care about.*

___ *Your job directly fulfills your work-related goals. It does not create barriers to realizing your other goals.*

___ *You like the people you work with.*

___ *You are on a winning team that is having a great time getting the job done.*

___ *A day on the job leaves you feeling energized, not burned out.*

Which of the unchecked statements do you want to have in your future career? Write them in your journal.

## CAREER VISUALIZATION

What work have you done in the past that was fulfilling in ways that are missing in your current career choice? Think back and notice what made it so satisfying. If you have not had a satisfying job before now, take a minute and imagine what it would be like. Close your eyes and visualize yourself in a career you love. Make it as real as possible. Try to actually see, feel, and hear yourself in the midst of working happily at this new job. Write about what it would be like to have a career that fits you perfectly.

Every part of your life is directly impacted by how your career fits you. People who work at fulfilling, challenging careers are more successful than people who are not passionate about what they do. They are healthier, live longer, and seem to be more satisfied with other parts of their lives. It is up to you to explore who you are and find an authentic career that fits you like a glove.

*This page adapted from* The Pathfinder *by Nicholas Lore*

# THE CHANGING WORLD OF WORK

by Keri Kurlinski-Walters

Aristotle has said, "Where your talents meet the needs of the world, therein lies your vocation." Therefore, it is important to understand the current world of work as you think about beginning your job search process.

Here we will illustrate the differences between the previous generation's world of work and your own. You will recognize the need to make your own decisions about work and to be ready to possibly change jobs or modify your career in the future. As the pace of our world of work becomes faster and faster, a broad knowledge base and flexibility become key skills for marketable employees.

Before reading the following, consider for yourself what some of the differences may be between your parents' world of work and your own. What about the world of work is different now than it was twenty years ago? Think about how the new world of work is changing, and what skills will be important to gain employment now and remain successfully employed in the future.

In some ways, today's world of work is exciting and challenging, and there are more opportunities for all people. But in other ways, doesn't it sometimes seem like your parents had it so much easier?

## Technology

When dear old dad learned his trade, he was most likely trained to use certain pieces of equipment or technology. The successful completion of this training meant that he could find work in that field. If he wanted to be an engineer, he studied engineering. If he wanted to be a washer and dryer repairman, he learned how to do that. Specific training led to a specific job. Today's world isn't so straightforward.

*The biggest mistake you can make is to believe that you work for someone else.*

UNKNOWN

Today, students earn B.A.s in things like Sociology, Philosophy, and English. And these same students work in business, communications, and government organizations. How and why does this happen? Well, employers understand that in the work world of today, technology is changing so quickly in every field that they need to invest lots of dollars in training programs for their employees to keep them up to speed. Since they are already investing so much money in training programs, hiring an employee who knows a particular technological skill becomes not as important as hiring an employee who knows how to learn things quickly. We are talking here about tangible versus intangible skills. Tangible skills are those technological things you may know

*The future belongs to those who prepare for it.*

RALPH WALDO EMERSON

*If you have built castles in the air, your work need not be lost; that is where they should be. Now put the foundations under them.*

HENRY DAVID THOREAU

how to do, like Microsoft Word, Photoshop, and other computer skills, for example. The thing to remember about tangible skills is they become obsolete very quickly as new technology comes on the market. Intangible skills are those things that employers can't teach you, but that you hopefully developed during college. These include things like oral and written communication skills, leadership skills, critical thinking skills, etc. So remember: unlike dad, you may look outside of your college major for job leads. Your employers will be happy to train you on the technological skills needed to do the job, as long as you have the intangible skills they are looking for.

## Marketability

A lot of people are earning college degrees, more than ever before. According to the National Center for Educational Statistics, between 1987-88 and 1997-98, associate degrees increased 28 percent, bachelor's degrees increased 19 percent, master's degrees increased 44 percent, and doctor's degrees increased 32 percent. This means that, unlike when mom and dad graduated from college, there is a lot more competition amongst the professional trades.

## Race and Gender

Although American women still only make around seventy-two cents on a man's dollar in the work force, we are here to stay. The economy depends on it. The U.S. Department of Labor Women's Bureau reports that between 1964 and 1999, for every two jobs added in government and sales for men, five were added for women in government and three were added for women in sales. During this same time period, four million women were added in education jobs. As a matter of fact, women's jobs at least doubled in every industry except manufacturing, while men's jobs only doubled in services, retail trade, and finance. Can you imagine if women were now taken out of the workforce? It would cripple our nation and the world. It's strange to think that women were not such an integral part of the world of work just a couple of generations ago.

There is also much greater diversity in our workforce than there was when our parents began their careers. What does diversity mean? It can mean many things, but we are speaking here about multicultural diversity. Many employers are now focused on increasing the diversity among their employees to more closely reflect the general population.

The workforce is full of so many more people than it was when our parents began their job search. Any type of job is open to anyone, increasing competition and also the quality of our products.

## Job Search Strategy

People used to send out lots of resumes and respond to job leads in the newspaper. This was sufficient in landing a job. Most of us need to be a lot more aggressive these days. The strategies used by our parents are no longer applicable. Nowadays, networking is key. Holding an internship is the number one way students right out of college get hired. You will also want to attend professional meetings in the field you hope to enter. Just expect the search process to be very different from your parents'!

## Loyalty and Movement

Interview your parents. Ask them how long they remained at their first job. If they're like my dad, they only ever had one job! Employees were expected to be loyal to the organization. If your parents had a lot of short term jobs on their resumes, they were probably asked, "why?" by interviewers. This is no longer true! It is perfectly acceptable and expected that employees will move around and do what's best for themselves career-wise. As more companies became less loyal to their employees, with layoffs and so forth, employees began to adopt the attitude of saving their own skin.

*I am living so far beyond my income that we may almost be said to be living apart.*

e. e. cummings

Now try telling mom or dad that you got a new position and it's a lateral move. You may hear, "What? Why on earth would you accept a lateral move?" People move laterally all the time now. There may be various reasons why you might want to do this. The lateral move may offer you something you want, like a shorter commute or additional benefits. Or, it may be a position where you can learn more on the job. In some cases, people even accept a lesser salary or a lesser amount of responsibility in their work in order to enter a new field. Whatever your reasoning, know that it is a perfectly acceptable thing to do, but also a relatively new development in the world of work.

*The article talks about "tangible" and "intangible" skills. What is the difference between them? What might be some examples of your own "tangible" and "intangible" skills?*

*How might your parents' experience of work and how to search for it differ from your own experience and expectations?*

*What piece of information most stood out for you from the article and why?*

*What might be some job search strategies that occur to you as a result of reading the article?*

## WORK ENVIRONMENTS

Before you begin searching for job leads, consider that there are many different ways to perform the career you have selected. For example, a graphic designer may work for a large corporation, at a cubicle-style office, supervising other graphic designers and making sure they maintain the company's graphic identity. Or, that same graphic designer might choose to be a freelancer, marketing himself or herself to clients and working from home, with more creative freedom. Your work environment has just as much or perhaps more to do with personal happiness as does the actual career itself.

When thinking about work environment, it is important to consider your own personality style and recognize what you want from your work. Take a look at the adjoining lists of personality characteristics at work. It is important to remember that there are no "good" or "bad" work styles listed below. Be honest with yourself about what kind of work situation you will be happiest in. You'll thank yourself later!

Place a check mark by the phrases that describe you.

## What gives you energy at work?

Do you....

| | |
|---|---|
| *Like variety and action* | *Like quiet for concentration* |
| *Tend to be fast* | *Tend to be careful* |
| *Like greeting people* | *Have trouble with names* |
| *Like the telephone* | *Dislike telephone interruptions* |
| *Act quickly, sometimes without thinking* | *Think a lot before action* |
| *Like to have lots of people around* | *Work contentedly alone* |
| *Communicate freely* | *Communicate only after thinking* |

If you checked more phrases on the left, look for a work environment that offers you lots of interaction with people and variety. If you checked more phrases on the right, look for a work environment that offers you your own quiet space and not a lot of interruptions.

## How do you prefer to take in information at work?

Do you....

| | |
|---|---|
| *Focus on the here and now* | *Focus on the future* |
| *Rely on tried and true ways to solve problems* | *Like solving problems in new ways* |
| *Like an established order of doing things* | *Dislike doing the same thing always* |
| *Enjoy using skills already learned* | *Like learning new skills on the job* |
| *Work steadily* | *Work in bursts of energy* |
| *Reach conclusion step by step* | *Come to understanding quickly* |
| *Become patient with routine details* | *Become impatient with routine details* |
| *Dislike complex situations* | *Welcome complex situations* |
| *Rarely trust your inspirations* | *Follow your inspirations* |
| *Seldom make factual errors* | *Sometimes make errors of detail* |
| *Like precise work* | *Dislike taking time for precision* |
| *Create by adapting something* | *Create something brand new* |

If you checked more phrases on the left, look for a work environment where you will work with factual and detailed information. If you checked more phrases on the right, look for a work environment where you can use your imagination and have a wide variety of tasks.

# How do you prefer to make decisions at work?

Do you....

| | |
|---|---|
| *Like analysis and logical order* | *Like harmony* |
| *Get along fine without harmony* | *Need harmony to function well* |
| *Tend to be firm minded* | *Tend to be sympathetic* |
| *Tend to be uncomfortable with feelings* | *Tend to be aware of others' feelings* |
| *Sometimes hurt others without knowing it* | *Enjoy pleasing other people* |
| *Make decisions impersonally* | *Make decisions personally* |
| *Need to be treated fairly* | *Need praise and personal attention* |
| *Reprimand people impersonally* | *Dislike/avoid giving criticism* |
| *Respond more to thoughts* | *Respond more to values* |

If you checked more phrases on the left, look for a work environment that calls for objective, impersonal decision making. If you checked more phrases on the right, look for a warm work environment with friendly people who appreciate you and offer positive feedback.

# How do you prefer to organize your work?

Do you....

| | |
|---|---|
| *Like to plan your work and follow your plan* | *Adapt well to change* |
| *Like things settled and finished* | *Prefer leaving things open* |
| *Decide things quickly* | *Unduly postpone decisions* |
| *Dislike interrupting projects for emergencies* | *Start too many projects without finishing* |
| *Feel satisfied once you reach conclusion* | *Remain open to new information* |

If you checked more phrases on the left, look for a work environment that is scheduled and organized, with a focus toward completing tasks. If you checked more phrases on the right, look for a work environment that is focused on change and is flexible.

*Adapted from the MBTI Manual, 3d ed., by Briggs Myers, McCaulley, Quenk, and Hammer*

## what is
# networking?

### unit two

*Objective: Understand and participate in a variety of networking opportunities.*

**NEW WAYS TO NETWORK**

**NETWORKING TIPS**

**HOW DO YOU NETWORK?**

**INFORMATIONAL INTERVIEWING**

**BUSINESS CARD TIPS**

**INTERVIEW SOMEONE IN YOUR FIELD**

## WHAT IS NETWORKING?

*Objective: Understand and participate in a variety of networking opportunities.*

**N**etworking means different things to different people. You may want to pause for a moment and consider what associations you make with networking. Some people may have negative connotations. This section may expand your understanding. Here you will be exposed to a variety of networking experiences, all intended to increase your knowledge of the field you plan to enter professionally.

You may find this article from the *Chicago Tribune* helpful in describing why networking is an absolute necessity in the job-searching process.

# New ways to network

adapted from a *Chicago Tribune* article

## What is networking?

By networking, we simply mean utilizing people and/or professional associations to gather career-related information. There are many different ways to do this.

Networking doesn't have to be done in person. E-mail and the telephone are also excellent ways to network. However, if you will be meeting someone in person, you will want to make the right impression. Networking should never be used to ask someone for a job, but it may serendipitously lead to a job in the future.

### NETWORKING TIPS

Joining professional associations is a great way to become more involved in your field. There are professional organizations in most fields, and most have reduced student annual fees. You cannot afford to not join one of these! Most organizations hold monthly meetings and/or annual conferences. If you are shy, take a friend with you or volunteer with the organization. At a conference, volunteering to check people in at the start of the day is a great way to get to meet people. And organizations are always looking for volunteers!

Always be ready to talk about what you want from your work. You never know when you will meet someone in your field who can help you. For tips on how to prepare for this type of conversation, see the section in this chapter on interviewing skills.

by Jean A. Williams

The saying goes: it's not what you know, it's who you know. But these days when it comes to networking for college students, there's a new twist on that well-worn phrase for graduates or soon-to-be college graduates.

"Something that we always tell students is it's not who you know, it's who knows you," said Keith Lusson, Director of the Career [Center for Arts & Media] at Columbia College. "Who's aware of what you want and what you can do? If nobody is aware of that, it's very difficult for you to find employment through more traditional methods: sending out your resume or pounding the pavement."

Even the lingo of networking has changed. Students are as likely to surf the Net as they are to pound the pavement for their first real gig.

One thing that hasn't changed, however, is the value of on-the-job experience, which for students translates into internships. That's the route that has proven fruitful for Todd Holfacker, who graduated last June from Columbia College with a bachelor's degree in Broadcast Journalism. Networking strategies were especially crucial for Holfacker, who decided as a junior that he was more interested in film than in journalism.

Holfacker met Bob Blinn [at Columbia] and found help in his film pursuits. "He basically told me that if this is what you want to do, then I will guide you," Holfacker said.

Holfacker applied for the Kodak American Pavilion Program in Cannes, France, and was chosen. Psyched by that experience, he hit the ground running upon his return to the States. "I got motivated and decided that I would find out all the different avenues in Chicago that dealt with the film industry," he said. He also checked out the local trades and joined different organizations.

His efforts are paying off. Holfacker moved to Los Angeles last fall and took a non-paying internship with Dreamworks Studios which he has since parlayed into a paying job with Reveal Entertainment, which has a first-look deal with Dreamworks.

●

But students must take the initiative, said Columbia College's Lusson. For some, such a simple thing can be quite intimidating.

"It's usually a personality thing, where someone isn't really comfortable, working a room," Lusson said. "That's either something that they're going to have to overcome or find some other way to enter the field."

Lucky for...Columbia students that their campuses are downtown or concentrated downtown, so taking initiative can be as simple as striking up a conversation with the right person, perhaps on the train to work.

"It's a little bit different than if you're down in Champaign," Lusson said. "You're sort of away from the city and away from the companies that you aspire to work for. Students who go to Columbia are literally blocks away from the museums, the art galleries, the ad agencies. We tell them to take advantage of their geographic location while they're in school."

As well, Lusson added, Columbia's faculty is comprised of instructors who work as hard in their disciplines as they do in their classrooms.

"We obviously encourage students to use the contacts that they make through teachers," he said. "There's more that this person can offer them than simply [lessons] in the classroom. Students can pick their brains or set up informational interviews to find out a little bit more about what's going on in the industry."

●

**?**

*What specific networking methods did Todd Holfacker use? What other types of networking opportunities are mentioned in the article?*

*For those of you who are presently employed, how did you find your current job? Was there any networking involved?*

*What networking have you done in the past? Was it successful? Why or why not?*

## HOW DO YOU NETWORK?

Many people hear the word "networking" and automatically assume that they will need to schmooze up a storm at some fancy party, being insincere and schmaltzy with strangers, trying to land a job. Not so. In fact, we recommend that you not do this. It is annoying and it usually doesn't work anyway.

There are, in reality, many different ways to network. The following exercise is designed to help you find the networking method that best fits your personality style. Look at the list below, and put a check mark in the appropriate column. Different personality types are drawn to different networking strategies. Use this worksheet to help determine some comfortable strategies for you.

| | I would definitely do this | I might consider doing this | I would never do this |
|---|---|---|---|
| Calling an acquaintance for an informational interview | ___ | ___ | ___ |
| Calling a stranger referred to you by an acquaintance | ___ | ___ | ___ |
| Cold calling someone in your field of interest | ___ | ___ | ___ |
| Talking with a career counselor | ___ | ___ | ___ |
| Attending a workshop in your field | ___ | ___ | ___ |
| Participating in an Internet chat room in your field of interest | ___ | ___ | ___ |
| Volunteering | ___ | ___ | ___ |
| Engaging in part-time work | ___ | ___ | ___ |
| Shadowing someone at work for a day | ___ | ___ | ___ |
| Completing an internship | ___ | ___ | ___ |
| Joining a professional association and attending a meeting | ___ | ___ | ___ |
| Conducting an informational interview through e-mail | ___ | ___ | ___ |

## INFORMATIONAL INTERVIEWING

# Informational interviewing is one of the most useful and typical ways of networking, so we will pay special attention to it here. You can conduct an informational interview by phone, e-mail, or face-to-face, whatever is most convenient for the person you are interviewing.

The goal of an informational interview is to obtain specific information about a field. It is not to get a job, although sometimes it may lead to one. You should never use an informational interview to ask for a position. This is in very poor taste.

Here are some things for you to decide before you arrange your informational interview.

*What do I want to know? Determine what information you are seeking. Do you want to know how a person's time is spent at work in a particular position? Are you more interested in a specific company and what it is like to work there? Do you need advice on how to get started in your field? Write out some sample questions below that you would like to get answered:*

*Who has the information I am looking for? You may have a mentor, faculty member, or friend of the family who has this information. If not, start asking people for a referral. Your faculty or career center may be able to set you up with a mentor or an alumnus to speak with. Write down some options of people to interview below:*

## BUSINESS CARD TIPS

Always remember to collect business cards of the people you meet with. This will serve two purposes: first, you can save the cards and contact people again in the future. Second, if the people you are meeting are taking time out of their day specifically for you, you will definitely want to write them a thank-you note. See the section on job search correspondence in this chapter for tips and sample thank-you notes.

Wear pockets to networking events for easy collection of business cards. Bring your own cards along as well to distribute. Even if you are still a full-time student, you can make your own business cards on the computer for a very low cost. Make sure to include your name, address, telephone number, and e-mail address on your card. Also include the line of work or profession you wish to enter, such as graphic designer or videographer.

Save your business cards in a safe and organized place, such as a rolodex, or enter them into a computer address program. Make notes on each card so you can remember a little bit about the person, such as when and where you met them and why you kept their card.

# Now you are ready to set up your informational interview. The following are some suggested ways of asking for the interview from Columbia College Chicago's Marketing Communication Department:

*"I was speaking with [name of person who referred you] the other day and he/she suggested I contact you. I'm in the process of making some important career changes and he/she felt that you might be able to give me some valuable advice. My purpose in requesting a brief meeting with you isn't to ask for a position, I don't expect you to have or even know of an opening. My goal is to get some advice from you and some insights into your field."*

●

*"I am in the process of making some important career decisions, and your advice would be extremely helpful. I am trying to learn more about the field of [your field here] to determine if it would be right for me. Your insights and experience will be very important as I make this decision. I would only need about thirty minutes of your time."*

●

*"I am currently in a job search process and I hoped I might get an opportunity to meet with you for thirty minutes or so. I do not want to ask you for a position. I don't expect you to have or even know of an opening. I would just like to share my strategy with you and hear any suggestions you might have. Is there a time in the next few weeks that is convenient for you?"*

●

These samples are suggestions to help you know what to ask when calling for an informational interview. Remember to use your own wording and personal style. These are only meant as guidelines and should not be read verbatim. You may even choose to use a combination of phrases you like from each sample.

## INTERVIEW SOMEONE IN YOUR FIELD

At a minimum, get answers to the following:

*How did you get started and how did you get to where you are today?*

*Is there anything you wish you had known before you entered the field?*

*What do you find most satisfying about your job? Least satisfying?*

*What are some of the most challenging situations you have faced in this job?*

*If you were a college student again, what would you do differently to prepare for your career?*

*What is currently available in the field?*

*How much demand is there for people in this career, and how can I make myself more marketable?*

*What kind of experience would you encourage for anybody pursuing a career in this field?*

*If you were conducting a job search today, how would you go about it?*

*Do you know of other people whom I might contact who have jobs similar to yours?*

job

search

correspondence

**RESUMES**

**ACCOMPLISHMENT INVENTORY**

**COVER LETTERS**

**THANK-YOU LETTERS**

unit three

*Objective: Prepare effective job search correspondence.*

# JOB SEARCH CORRESPONDENCE

*Objective: Prepare effective job search correspondence.*

I n Unit Three, we will discuss three main types of job search correspondence, what the purpose is of each, and how you can use them to display your best self to the employer. The three types of correspondence we will introduce are resumes, cover letters, and thank-you letters. This unit will give you some important things to consider when drafting your correspondence, but remember, it is not meant to replace the meaningful feedback you can receive by visiting your career center. It is always a good idea to have faculty and career advisors review your correspondence prior to sending it out.

## RESUMES

What is the purpose of the resume? Many people think the purpose of a resume is to get them a job. Not so. The purpose of the resume is to get you an *interview.* You want an employer to recognize your skills so that you might get a chance to meet with that employer and really sell yourself.

The first question most students ask is, "Do I need to put an objective on my resume?" You will get different opinions on this, so use your best judgment. If you do decide to use it, however, remember what the function of the objective is: it is to identify what job position you are applying for. It should be the first thing listed on your resume, right after your name and contact information. If you are applying for more than one job title, you should prepare a separate resume with a different objective for each job you are seeking. *It is imperative that your objective match the job title listed in the job lead.*

⁕

Remember, you don't necessarily need to use an objective. Fine artists and performing artists especially do not need an objective. If you are sending a resume but don't know what position titles are available, you definitely don't need an objective. See your career advisor if you are unsure.

Many college students feel that they don't have enough experience to create an impressive resume. Does this apply to you? Don't fear. We have the perfect solution for you: a section on your resume called the "Skills" section or "Professional Profile."

Before you create a Skills section on your resume, it is important to conduct a skills inventory for yourself. Set aside a quiet hour or so to complete this activity. List the skills you have in the following categories:

**SAMPLE OBJECTIVE STATEMENTS**
from the Career Center for Arts & Media at Columbia College:

*To contribute my growing skills and superior enthusiasm as an editing intern*

*To provide graphic solutions that integrate content with fresh, effective visual strategies as a graphic designer*

### Tangible Skills:

*Computer skills*

*Oral communication skills*

*Written communication skills*

*Management skills*

### Intangible Skills:

*Teamwork skills*

*Leadership skills*

*Critical thinking skills*

*Organizational skills*

Another way to think about skills is to think about the college courses you have taken and what you have learned in them. Some students list the courses they have taken directly on their resume, but we do not recommend this. Instead, turn those courses into skills. For example, if you took a class called Intro to Computer Graphics, list the skills you acquired from that course, e.g., Photoshop, Illustrator, and Flash. Next, prepare a short statement for your Skills section, e.g., "Proficient in Photoshop, Illustrator, and Flash."

Once you have completed your skills inventory, you are ready to prepare a Skills section or Professional Profile section for your resume. If you lack significant work experience in your field, we recommend putting the Skills section at the top of your resume. A Skills section is valuable for anyone because many employers now have software that reads the resume. The software will scan your resume for keywords, many of which will appear in your Skills section. Also, if you have a particular skill but haven't used it on the job yet, this is a great way to get it on your resume.

●

Now that you have your Skills section ready, you will need to include a section called Related Experience or something similar. Notice that this reads Related Experience and not Work Experience. You may have work experience that does not relate to the job you are applying for. This experience should not go on your resume. Likewise, you may have unpaid experience that is related to the job you are applying for. This experience should go on your resume.

**SAMPLE SKILLS**

Here is an example of a Skills section for a graduating senior:

*Proficient in Microsoft Word, Filemaker Pro, Internet and e-mail usage, and Excel*

*Strong written and oral communicator with a polished presentation style*

*Effective manager and trainer*

*Proven organizer with a strong work ethic and good attention to detail*

As you can see, this student uses a combination of both tangible and intangible skills in her Skills section.

## ACCOMPLISHMENTS INVENTORY

To determine the wealth of items you have to place under this section, it is often helpful to complete an accomplishments inventory. An accomplishment is an activity in which you have done a good job, feel a sense of pride in having done it, and enjoyed doing it.

List a minimum of three specific examples that you think represent accomplishments and relate to the type of job you are seeking. In your examples, list the action(s) you took to solve the problem(s) and the results that could be seen, or even better, measured. Use experiences in which you truly enjoyed yourself, both paid and unpaid. Some of your accomplishments may have taken place at a job, internship, or volunteer opportunity in your field. Others of your accomplishments may have taken place as a group project for class. Whatever the case, this exercise is important in brainstorming your Related Experience section for your resume.

*Name of Organization*

*Title/Position Held*

*Situation (What situation, task, or problem needed solving?)*

*Action (What action did you take?)*

*Result (What was the result of your actions? Quantify results whenever possible.)*

Now that you have completed your Related Experience section, it is important to be aware of the different types of resumes you will need to have on hand. Your resume should be geared specifically toward the type of job you are applying for, so you may need several different resumes with slightly different content, depending on the focus of the job. You will also be asked to relay your resume to the potential employer via different methods. Here are some of the methods you will be asked to use:

Snail mail: When sending a resume through snail mail, you can feel free to be as fancy as you like. If you like to use colored resume paper, go for it. If you want to include icons or designs on your resume (especially helpful for graphic designers), do so. Always include a cover letter (covered in the next section) with your resume. This type of resume is also good to take along with you to an interview, or to drop off in person.

Fax: A faxable resume is a bit different. Scrap the colored paper for this. You will need to use a resume on white paper to make sure it turns out correctly on the other end. Scrap the icons and fancy designs as well; these seldom reproduce correctly on the other end of a fax machine. Do make sure you have at least a one-inch margin on all sides of the faxable resume so that no text gets cut off. Send a cover letter with the faxable resume, again being certain there are one-inch margins on all sides.

E-mail: This is becoming the most common method for sending your resume, and also the most confusing. You will not be able to include designs or even format in this type of resume. Your e-mail resume should be sent in plain text, with the resume content in the body of the e-mail itself. Do not send your resume as an attachment; most employers will not even open it because of the risk of computer viruses. Even if an employer does venture to open your attachment, chances are their fonts and programs will be different, and your resume will not look as you intended it to look anyway. So, sending it in plain text and in the body of the e-mail is best. You may also include a cover letter in this manner.

Personal Website: Want to really impress an employer? Direct him/her to your personal Website. You can create your own Website very cheaply, and this is a very effective and impressive job-seeking tool. On your Website you can include your resume, samples of your work, and references. Include your Website address on all other correspondence, including other types of resumes and cover letters you send.

Remember, your resume is important. It is a reflection of you, your skills, your interests, and your values. For more tips on resume writing, see your career advisor in the Career Center for Arts & Media. He/she can help you edit your resume and sort out what is important to include.

## COVER LETTERS

# The cover letter accompanies your resume when marketing yourself to a prospective employer.

Much attention is given to the design and content of your resume, and duly so. Yet in many ways, the cover letter is just as important, if not more so. The cover letter is the first piece of communication the prospective employer sees from you. It is written in a freer, more conversational style than the resume, and can allow you an opportunity to communicate your individuality on paper. It does not repeat information already held in the resume, but highlights your most valuable experiences.

**Anatomy of a Cover Letter:** The first paragraph of your cover letter should be a simple greeting. It should state the position you are applying for and where you found out about the opportunity. You should also express your enthusiasm in this first paragraph, but keep it short: two to three sentences, tops.

The second paragraph is where you highlight the experiences on your resume that are particularly applicable to the position for which you are applying. Think about not only the work and educational experiences you have had, but also where you had them. For example, if applying for a design position with a nonprofit organization, think about the nonprofit organizations on your resume and highlight those. Find out what the employer values and highlight the similar values that you espouse. This is the paragraph where you really sell yourself and get the employer to read on!

In the third paragraph, thank the employer for the time he/she took in reading your letter. Give your contact information (your phone number and e-mail address). Mention that you look forward to talking with them soon.

# Don't forget to sign your cover letter!

# Make sure your contact information is current. Make sure you have an answering machine. Check your e-mail every day!

# Always use active, rather than passive, verbs. (Example: "I completed seven courses in design" rather than "seven courses were completed in design.")

# Scan the job lead for the specific skills the employer is looking for. Use your cover letter to prove that you have those skills.

# See your career advisor for answers to any specific questions you may have.

# Remember, do not add random information that does not relate to the job lead. When communicating one of your values, make sure you tie it back to how it will benefit the employer. This will get you a winning cover letter!

## THANK-YOU LETTERS

# Thank-you letters are a crucial follow-up to any interview situation, whether it be a job interview or an informational interview. The thank-you letter offers you the opportunity to display your professionalism as well as remind the employer of your enthusiasm for the position.

Thank-you letters can be mailed, faxed, or e-mailed. Time is of the essence. Make sure you send a thank-you letter immediately following any interview situation. Thank-you letters should always be typed. Stay clear of handwritten notes unless the interview was extremely casual.

Send a thank-you letter to everyone you met with during the interview. Make sure to collect business cards of everyone present. You will be glad you did later, when you have to spell all of their names correctly!

**Anatomy of a Thank-you Letter:** Thank-you letters should be brief and to the point. In the first paragraph, simply thank the employer for taking the time to get to know you as a candidate. Let him/her know that you enjoyed the conversation.

In the second paragraph, think of something that particularly excited you about the interview, and mention it here. For example, "The brochure you want to develop is very exciting to me." Then, follow up with a statement of what you will bring to that particular project. For example, "I am confident that my skills as a designer and illustrator, as well as my enthusiasm for your goals and mission, will serve you well in this endeavor." In this way, you are letting the employer know that you are still excited about the prospect of working with him or her after the interview. You are also reiterating your skills and qualification for the position.

In the third paragraph, simply state your contact information, including telephone and e-mail address, and thank the employer once again for their time.

## If for some reason

you find you are no longer interested in the position following the interview, it is important that you still send a thank-you note. However, you will need to follow a different format. The first paragraph can remain the same, but in the second paragraph you will want to remove yourself from the candidate pool in a kind and diplomatic way. Perhaps the position or employer was not a good fit for you. Find a way to explain this in a way that does not burn bridges for you. The employer will appreciate your honesty and professionalism.

# job search
# strategies
## and interviewing

*Objective: Explore job search strategies and prepare for successful, professional interviews.*

## unit four

## JOB SEARCH STRATEGIES AND INTERVIEWING

*Objective: Explore job search strategies and prepare for successful, professional interviews.*

You already know how to conduct informational interviews and research your career interests. You know the names of the job titles and work functions, along with details such as salary ranges and skill sets required. You understand the industries you're trying to break into, know who the hiring managers are, and can name the types of employers and companies. You've assessed where you want to fit into your career field—you know what you want to do, where you want to do it, and what you have to offer.

Now, you've got to find out where the job openings and other work opportunities are, so you can go ahead and apply. But first, brace yourself: your search is probably going to be an exciting, scary, exhilarating, and mystifying ride.

# FINDING JOB OPENINGS AND OPPORTUNITIES

By Paula Brien, Career Advisor, Career Center for Arts & Media, Columbia College Chicago

## Where the Jobs Are

Two types of job openings are out there: ones you know about before you approach an employer—those are the ones that are advertised in newspapers or on the Web or which came to you by way of a friend's tip, and the ones you don't—those are the ones where you approach an employer with your fingers crossed that he or she's got an opening (or will have shortly).

## I Want a Job!

To find as many job leads and potential employers to approach as possible, put the word out that you're looking. It's best if you're specific. Test this out [fill in the blanks]:

"I'm looking for a job as a _____ with a _____.
My major was _____, and I've got a bit of experience in
_____ through _____."

You can create a few versions of this statement, depending on how many career options you're considering. Such a statement will help attract tips of actual job leads, names of likely employers, and referrals to useful resources such as industry e-mail listservs and niche job listings publications.

## THE BASICS OF JOB SEARCHING: TALKING AND READING

**Coffee Talk:** Are you really comfortable chatting with people? If so, then talking to people is the best way for you to start getting the word out about your job search. You can do this face-to-face, over the phone, through direct e-mails, and through e-mail listservs and Internet bulletin boards. Know your protocol (a.k.a. "manners"), however, before you jump into these "conversations." You can brush up on ever-evolving standards of protocol by asking your college instructors, internship advisors, career advisors, classmates, and others who have friendly relationships with you to fill you in.

Ultimately, with all talking, you aim to speak to the person in the hiring seat at your "wish list" employers.

**Be Bookish:** Reading is also an important way to find job leads—this includes the obvious, such as reading the weekly Sunday help-wanted classified ads (on-line or in print), as well as scouring trade magazines for subtle hints about which employers are likely in a hiring mood.

Read newspapers, magazines, and even the flyers tacked on those cork bulletin boards featured in every college building. You're looking for announcements of job openings, but you're also looking for the off-beat information and roundabout ways of learning of leads.

## GO ROUNDABOUT

Here's a list of the roundabout ways of finding job openings—this is sometimes called the "hidden" job market:

Read the business news (in the *Chicago Tribune* and *Sun-Times*, the *Daily Southtown*, the *Daily Herald*, and *Crain's Chicago Business*, as well as professional, industry, and trade newsletters and magazines). Feel free to ask your career advisor in the college's Career Center for Arts & Media what news sources you could be monitoring to learn about new ventures, job fairs, personnel changes, and other tidbits that could point to a potential job opening.

Read people-on-the-move columns in trade publications. ("Hey, maybe that organization needs a new assistant, too.") ("Hey, a lot seems to be happening at that company.")

Read e-mail listservs and Internet bulletin boards (but scope their purpose first—because these are interactive, you might be permitted to post questions about job openings and your target employers).

Here are other important, but "backdoor," ways of gaining entry to a company or organization:

- *introductions to the employer by other people*

- *through your internship with the company or organization*

- *by taking assignments with the company from placement and temp agencies (as new professionals, you're not ready for headhunters yet)*

- *by freelancing for the company or organization*

- *by volunteering for the company or with nonprofit organization alongside the company's representatives*

- *by attending conventions where you can meet the employer*

- *by "job shadowing" a professional in your industry for a day*

- *taking road trips to the employers' location (think: New York City, L.A., D.C., etc.)*

- *securing a grant and then bringing it with you to a nonprofit employer*

## HOW TO SUBMIT YOUR STUFF

When you're ready to approach an employer and ask for a job, answer these questions of yourself first: Are you applying for a known, open job? Or, are you prospecting for openings with an employer you might want to work for? Each case tends to require a different approach.

The typical approach for known openings is to submit a cover letter, tailored resume, and work samples. (Or, you could wait until you follow up with the employer when he or she requests your work samples before you submit those. Follow the conventions of your industry.)

On the other hand, when you're trying to start a relationship with a prospective employer and you have no idea if there's any job open, your approach could be a phone call, letter, or e-mail. It's your decision, based on what you think he or she will be receptive to.

And you do have many choices of how to submit your materials, ranging from in-person drop-off to filling out an on-line form. Thankfully, most employers will tell you exactly how they want it. Usually any job ad will describe the required process, but when you're prospecting for unknown openings with an employer, do some background research such as calling their human resources administrative assistant to ask how the company prefers to receive inquiries about job openings.

## EXTRA STUFF

**Salary History and/or Salary Requirements:** If the employer asks job applicants to include a salary history and/or salary requirements, consider placing this information in sentence form within the second to the last paragraph of your cover letter. Consider being fairly vague, because you as yet don't know the details of the job duties and their pay scale. How about something along the lines of: "My past wages have reflected competitive rates for student employment and internships, and my annual salary requirement ranges from the mid to high $20,000s depending on the nature and requirements of the XYZ position you are seeking to fill." (Of course, your answers are based on the research you've done into salaries for your industry.)

**References:** Usually, you never send these until they are specifically requested. You, of course, can drop names of any meaningful references in your cover letter—in the first sentence, even. What are friends for, anyway?

**Work samples:** In the arts and communications field, we're asked to show what we can do as part of the job search. In terms of what to show, how to show it, when to show it, you must know what the convention is for the types of positions you're seeking. Feel free to discuss this with your career advisor in the college's Career Center for Arts & Media.

**RECOMMENDED READING**

Compiled by Career Advisors of the Career Center for Arts & Media, Columbia College Chicago

Information Interviewing: *How to Tap Your Hidden Job Market,* 2d ed., (October 1996), by Martha Stoodley

*How to Work a Room: The Ultimate Guide to Savvy Socializing in Person and Online,* rev. ed. (December 2000), by Susan RoAne

*Job Searching Online for Dummies,* 2d ed. (January 2000), by Pam Dixon

*Writing Resumes, Cover Letters, and Other Essential Materials for Jobs in Arts and Media,* published by the Career Center for Arts & Media, Columbia College Chicago. (Free to Columbia College Chicago students and alumni.)

*Negotiating Your Salary: How to Make $1,000 a Minute* (June 2001), by Jack Chapman

**Employment Applications:** By the way, if you are asked to interview, be prepared to fill out a formal employment application as part of the process—many times, it's required. So, have employment details like phone numbers of former employers on hand—just in case. Frequently these applications ask you to describe the "reason for leaving" a position. This is not the time to drag the name of your former supervisor through the mud. Rather, practice discretion and positive spin and state something along the lines of: "left to find employment closer to my college campus, so I could spend more hours in the school's photo lab" or something equally benign.

## MARCHING TO A DIFFERENT DRUMMER ON THE PATH LESS FOLLOWED

Some employers and industries have ways of finding employees that differ from what we've just been talking about. For example, students seeking advertising copywriting jobs are frequently asked to "drop" their "book" off at the ad agency for review and to pick it up a week later—never having even interviewed for a job or learning if there is a job opening. The lucky ones get asked in for an interview based on the impression their books made. And, of course, stage actors must watch for audition notices and be available to attend the auditions when they're looking for work—they don't send resumes first.

Here, career advisors from Columbia College's Career Center for Arts & Media offer details needed by students pursuing unique paths to paid work:

## Q: I'm a broadcast production student. Should I try to join a union when I graduate to help me find jobs?

A: [Doug Bonner, broadcast Career Advisor] For radio, video, and TV industry production it's not a good idea for students to go out and join a union while they're still building their resume. Becoming a union worker entails several concerns, such as: Will the union's executive board accept their application? and Can they pay the four-figure initiation fee?

Perhaps the most important reason is that it will keep fresh graduates ineligible from working on nonunion productions in positions which could build their resume. Also, as a new union member, grads won't have any seniority on the union roster; and therefore, will be the last ones hired. As a result, recent grads would be paying a four-figure sum for the opportunity of sitting around waiting for the phone to ring—an opportunity the rest of the world is glad to provide gratis.

The standard scenario for hooking up with a union is that one gets a job at a union shop and then joins the local. After working for several years at the shop and deciding that one wants to freelance, he or she will have enough seniority to be high up on the roster for frequent day hires.

However, Columbia students and grads are fortunate in that the National Academy of Television Arts and Sciences (NATAS) has open membership. The Chicago chapter of this professional organization does not require a certain number of years in the industry as a prerequisite for membership (the average at other chapters seems to be about three years of cumulative experience in legitimate broadcast endeavors). So, I would encourage you to get involved with NATAS.

## Q: I want to work as "talent" in radio and television. Should I get an agent?

A: [Doug Bonner, broadcast Career Advisor] In Chicago, most agent duties are handled by attorneys. Having an agent is only advantageous if you are doing voice-over work. Otherwise, the attorney hammers out the contract. (Even then, it's usually only established talent who employ the services of attorneys.)

## Q: I'm a photography major. How can I get paid for my professional work?

A: [Tim Long, photography Career Advisor] Most photography jobs are done by "freelance" photographers. That means the photographer is an independent worker, not an employee of a company. So, rather than jumping into full-time freelancing, you might want to start out as an assistant to a photographer—that way you can learn the ropes of running your own business, as well as develop your professional photography skills on the job. Eventually, you'll have the confidence—and experience—to strike out on your own.

## Q: I want a career on stage. What now?

A: [Will Casey, performing arts Career Advisor] Well, mainly you've got to stay informed about auditions. Check the performing arts trade magazines, hotlines, and Websites—actors, for example, read *PerformInk*, published every other Thursday, and *Audition News*, published monthly. Both of these have listings for other talent, but they are mostly audition notices for theater. The Casting Hotline (312.976.CAST) has recorded listings. Equity actors can call a hotline as well. "Triple-threat" talent (actor/singer/dancer) auditions are publicized through theater listings.

In addition, check the various informal "grapevines" and numerous bulletin board-type postings—these still seem to be the most common, short-notice way of publicizing job openings. In general, bulletin boards in rehearsal, class, and performance spaces are good places to check for postings. For instance: Act I Bookstore in Chicago has several well-read bulletin boards which are forever full of last-minute tech, casting, and production notices. Simply being in the habit of reading the bulletin board (as well as being lucky enough to be one of the first to respond to a new notice) can mean getting the job. Several bulletin boards in Columbia's Theater and Music departments operate on the same "first-come" basis.

Music and dance periodicals (mostly monthly) have numerous ads for "open" auditions for large companies or conservatories. Dancers generally work up through the ranks in schools and private classes, and move into dance companies through their teachers/choreographers. Typically, all performers' unions have hotlines for up-to-the-minute job opportunities.

## Q: OK, I'll be doing lots of auditions—but what do I need to know before I go?

A: [Will Casey, performing arts Career Advisor] You'll be watching for "open" auditions, the ones posted in various trade publications. Anyone with a headshot and resume can schedule an audition time, or just show at the posted times. Of course, most theaters feature a cast breakdown in their ad, so no one's time is wasted seeing people of the wrong age, race, or gender.

Every theater with an Equity contract has to make audition times available for union actors, whether the show is precast or not (with the "big" theaters, obviously, many leading roles are precast, either with ensemble members, local "stars," or out-of-towners. In this case, the union auditions are a mere formality, and a uniformly miserable experience for all involved!).

Most theaters also hold "season" auditions (with both union and "open" audition days), for actors to be considered for roles in the entire season. These usually feature the casting director, and possibly the directors of the shows. This is a good way for them to judge the existing talent pool.

The League of Chicago Theatres also sponsors the "Generals," where representatives of nearly all of Chicago's theaters attend several days of "cattle call" auditions, again, to look for new (nonunion) talent. It's a grueling process, as hundreds of actors participate, and theaters must deal with an influx of hundreds of new headshots and resumes (to say nothing of hundreds of substandard auditions!). Actors must apply for a spot in Generals; applications are usually available in theaters around the city and at Act I Bookstore by the end of March. Generals are in May or June.

By the way, the audition trade paper for New York is *Backstage*; for L.A., it is *Backstage West*, and these are both mainly for stage work. *Hollywood Reporter*, *Weekly Variety*, and *Daily Variety* are the trades for film. Film auditions are arranged entirely through casting directors contacting talent agencies, who then call actors in their talent pool matching the cast breakdowns. Actors generally meet these agents through a mailed submission of their headshot and resume, and invitation to current shows, or notice of upcoming film/television exposure.

# Q: Will I find a lot of entry-level film job openings posted on the Internet?

A: [Matt Green, associate film/video Career Advisor] In a word: No. Typically the Internet is a tough place to find entry-level work in film, video, and animation. Most general employment sites, like Monster.com, do not include extensive resources for these disciplines. Although there are many Websites dedicated specifically to creative and production work, generally they are geared toward mid- to senior-level freelance professionals and list mostly Los Angeles-based jobs. These sites include: www.entertainmentcareers.net, www.mandy.com, www.productionhub.com, and www.awn.com (which is Animation World Network).

Since jobs in film, video, and animation are mostly project based, the only reliable way to seek out work is to contact the production companies, individual production managers, and studios directly to see if or when they expect to have openings. There are numerous directory books and Websites out there to help you do this—some are free, some expensive. If you write and then call to follow up with the people and companies in these directories, you will have the best chance of finding entry-level work.

These are the best directory sources, if you are seeking work here in Chicago:

• *Illinois Production Guide* (Order a free copy of the guide by calling the Illinois Film Office at 312.814.3600.)

• *Chicago Creative Directory* (Bookmark it at www.creativedir.com.)

• *Screen Magazine's Production Bible* (Can be purchased—the 2002 price is $55—by calling 312.640.0800.)

Note that each discipline within film, video, and animation (i.e., editors, cinematographers, writers, animators) typically has its own directory. Directories are also published specific to most geographical areas. Places like Los Angeles and New York have numerous directories. Most states and larger cities publish free directories. Ask your teachers and search the Internet for the directory most relevant to your career path and where you live.

**SAY GOOD-BYE TO CHICAGO**

"Relocation" is the fancy word for taking your act on the road to work in another city, state, or country. A job search in Chicago is one thing, but a job search that might result in a relocation is a whole "'nuther ball of wax." Check with your alumni relations office to see if any Columbia alumni live in the area you're considering—an alumnus might extend a welcoming hand to you in your quest to relocate.

To find a job in another city, you can take two approaches:

*You can base your search from your home in the Chicago area and look for work in places yonder, or*

*You can move to the city where you want to work and then conduct your search from your new home.*

One of your major considerations: Where are you going to live, and how are you going to pay your bills during your job search? Another major consideration is whether someone from out of the area can fill the type of job you're seeking. Also, does the kind of employer you're targeting hire only people living in the immediate area?

Get the information before you make any big decisions. Again, find out from your industry connections what is typical for the jobs and employers you're seeking. Their answers can help you determine if you must move first and then look for work, as well as the best ways to do that.

# TIPS FOR MANAGING YOUR JOB SEARCH

Set up your regimen.

Manage the emotional highs and lows of your job search. There's a lot of weirdness out there waiting for you in the job market. Make sure you're safe—physically and emotionally. Accept the confusion and "limbo" that you may experience during this time. If you can stay clearheaded, you will be more likely to notice opportunities when they arise.

Line up some "stopgap" jobs to tide you over in case the job search stretches out longer than you had hoped. Where to look for stopgap jobs: temp agencies, paid postgraduate internships, community newspapers, substitute teaching.

Reality checks for when you aren't getting any interviews: Double check that you're targeting job openings and types of employers who match what you're bringing to the party. Assess this at regular intervals. If you are getting interviews, that's the best sign that you're a viable job candidate, and you're really playing a numbers game—where you have to have enough interviews to hit the one employer who decides to offer you the job. If you're always coming in number two, then consider asking each employer what swayed his or her decision. You might gain some useful intelligence from asking this question. It also can take the sting out of rejection.

Record keeping: Log your job search actions and list your "to dos." Set up a job search "control center" in your home—job searching is paper intensive and you have to be ready to respond to opportunities. Don't set yourself up where you'll have to riffle through disorganized piles to find a certain version of your resume or the name of the guy who interviewed you last Tuesday.

In a related vein, clean up your outgoing phone message so that it reflects you as a job candidate, not you-as-a-death-metal-music-fan (unless that's a big plus on the job).

Make sure you have a full "wardrobe" of stationery, faxing capability, and access to e-mail and the Internet. Keep postage stamps on hand. Have a library card and borrowing privileges. Also have a way of getting around: a car when you need it, airfare, bus fare.

Speaking of wardrobe, have about three complete sets of "interview" and "networking" clothes. Make sure the shoes work with the pants, the bag with the coat, etc. There are too many students and recent grads out there walking into interviews or professional association gatherings in sloppy, incomplete getups. Use all your considerable ingenuity to outfit yourself on a shoestring.

# Give yourself "time on task." If you're currently

unemployed and not busy with school, give your job search forty hours per week—yes, just like a full-time job. Use the other time to live your life, do laundry, go ice skating, learn to play the zither, visit your honey. If you spend part of your week doing schoolwork or at a part-time job, then conduct your job search in twenty hours per week. If you're in a full-time job or doing schoolwork full-time, then at least squeeze ten hours of job searching in per week. If you're in both school and working full-time, then God bless you. Do your job search when you can.

# Take a "layered" approach to ramping up your job

search. The first step of an active job search is to apply to job ads. The second layer is to begin to cold call companies. The third track to add is to start networking with professionals. And then after you've got a firm grip on that, start spinning the "freelancing" plate in the air. And keep them all spinning. The idea is to not overwhelm yourself immediately. Don't try to move to the next step until you've hit your stride in the previous step.

# How long should your job search last?

Realistically, a well-done search could last anywhere from one day to two years. Don't hyperventilate. Remember you're trying to break into a very competitive field and find a job that you'd really like, right? Be clear about what you are willing or unwilling to do. Please don't bail out too early. You will be fine-tuning your job search techniques and building knowledge throughout the whole ordeal. Typically, two months pass from the moment you send your resume responding to a single job opening, to the day you send your acceptance letter in response to a job offer.

# Have a spiel about yourself at the ready. Be able

to say, "I'm the one who…" that will fix you in people's memory. The more you are a unique person (don't read this as "a strange person") who stands out in people's minds, the better they are able to assist you.

# Hang out with the tribe—parties, bars, ball games,

twelve-step programs that attract a lot of people who already work in the industries you're most interested in—they're all places to talk about careers aspirations with like-minded folks. And you might have fun to boot.

# Let the spirit grab you. Infuse your job search with

"spirit." Approach it with a positive attitude, and don't slack off or drift into an ongoing negative mind-set. (This could cause you to not notice opportunities when they finally do arise.) During your job search, you will develop a reputation that will affect how people are willing to help you—or not.

**OTHER TIPS**

* If you decide to do a remote job search— where you stay put in Chicago—the Internet and on-line resources will be a big help. Use the industry on-line resources that focus only on the city you're targeting or use broad ones that include contacts from the city you're targeting.

* With a remote search, the challenge can come when you land an interview and need to find the time and funds to travel to it. (Stash some cash for this purpose.)

* If you have been applying for job openings but not getting any interviews, you might want to schedule a prospecting trip to the place you want to move. Try to arrange a visit with the employers before you arrive—sometimes you can get time with them as a courtesy.

The Inside Track to

# CREATIVE JOBS

The mainstays of a standard job search—want ads, Websites, human resource people, and recruiters—play only bit parts in most creative workers' quests for entry-level jobs. At all but the biggest ad agencies, design shops, and new media studios (among many other creative businesses) job seekers must interact directly with the artists and designers already at work.

In creative businesses the established workers are expected to bring forth new people in somewhat the same manner that old-style politicians selected new candidates. The smoke-filled back room may be replaced by a sun-and-fern-filled studio, but the process of locating new artistic talent happens internally and is reliant upon connections between people. Picture a design studio or agency creative department that has just landed a big new account or lost one of their artists and the need to hire an entry-level person has become clear. The following conversation might take place around a lunch table bristling with Chinese take-out cartons and chop sticks.

The Boss: *We got the go-ahead to hire someone. Green tea, anyone? So Bobby, you know anyone that can work for us?*

Bobby: *Saw a guy's portfolio last week. Nice work. Got a sense of humor. Will you be eating that egg roll, Charles, or what?*

The Boss: *Charles. Tell me who you'd like to take Susan's place, and pass the mustard sauce, would you?*

Charles: *I reviewed a young woman's book in the fall. She has talent and she's been keeping in touch. I'll forward her resume to you. Please be kind enough to remove your sleeve from my kung pow chicken, Bob.*

The Boss: *Elaine, did you get enough to eat? Hey, got anybody in mind for this job?*

Elaine: *Boss, I got a file full of resumes. Let me look at my notes and pull out the best of them.*

The Boss: *By tomorrow morning. We need the help. Say, if you're not going to finish that...*

By Tim Long
Career Advisor
Career Center for Arts & Media
Columbia College Chicago

The "nominated" candidates would be invited to interview. If a person surfaced from among these candidates that looked to fit, a second interview might follow or perhaps a couple days of freelancing would be offered. If all goes well, a job offer is made. If the offer is agreeable to the job candidate, take-out lunch orders are increased by one.

This person-to-person hiring strategy is, no doubt, responsible for the cynical saying, "It's not what you know, it's who you know." To the relief of many, this concept is entirely false, at least as it's commonly understood. First off, without a competitive portfolio that demonstrates what you know, you will get nowhere—period—end of story. Secondly, it's not who you know but who knows you that puts you in the running for entry-level creative work. Importantly, "knowing you" doesn't mean that you must be related to, are a former schoolmate of, or are owed a favor by those on the inside, though none of these connections hurt. It does mean that working artists and designers need to know you, professionally, via portfolio and interview, at the time they are hiring.

From the creative job seeker's perspective, this hiring system may seem entirely random and subjective. Understandably so. But from the creative employer's viewpoint, this method is eminently practical. Based on the traditionally safe assumption that there are far fewer creative jobs available than there are artists and designers to fill them, creative employers don't need to seek out new "talent." They simply let the talent come to them. This allows employers to sidestep both recruiting and the placement of want ads and the paper shuffling incurred by those actions. Another practical benefit of this hiring method is the informed evaluation of job candidates and their portfolios by established creative employees—something beyond the scope of "noncreative" human resource personnel. As suggested above, when the need to hire arises, creative employers can simply invite a handful of people who have already presented themselves and their portfolios to come in for what is, in effect, a second interview. It's easy (for them).

The upshot of all this is that the responsibility to check in with companies belongs to the creative job seeker and to that person alone. Creative employers won't magically summon you to interview the day after you've finished putting your portfolio together. And while mailing out resumes and waiting by the phone may get you caught up with the soaps, it's highly doubtful that it will get you enough interviews to get you the job you want. Also note that checking in with creative companies more often than not takes place well before a position is available.

Then who are the companies that do place job leads in the job section of the Sunday newspaper, career-related Websites, and college job boards? Most often they are companies off the beaten trail for creative job seekers: large corporations and small start-up creative consultants that because of their omnipresence or lack of presence, artists and designers often don't recognize as potential employers. (When you think of Amoco, you think of gasoline not Website design.) Since these businesses are not regularly approached by new talent, they may be unable to establish an adequate pool of creative people to draw from.

These "published" job leads may be worth your effort to follow up on. Why not? Someone will take those jobs. But it means that you'll be going resume to resume with unreasonably large numbers of other creative candidates. Not the best scenario for a portfolio driven job search. Much smarter is to position yourself on the inside track for job information and opportunity with artists and designers already at work for the companies that you, too, would like to work for.

Your instructor may take you through some mock interviews in class to help you prepare for the interviewing process. Here are some tips to help you get ready!

## INTERVIEWING TIPS

Research! Before the interview, it is imperative that you do as much research as possible about the company/organization you are interviewing with. This is essential so that you look polished during the interview, and so that you can prepare intelligent questions for the employer at the end of the interview.

Get a job description. The employer should provide you with a job description prior to the interview. If they do not, call their reception desk and ask to have one e-mailed or faxed to you.

Dress professionally. Again, do some research here and find out what is appropriate to wear. Try to ask someone in the same field for recommendations. If you cannot find out any information in this area, dress up. It is better to be overdressed than underdressed. Personal hygiene is also important. If it is a lunch interview, bring floss and don't order anything embarrassing, like a spinach salad, for example. Do not wear heavy perfumes or colognes.

Be respectful of people's time. Do not be late for an interview. It is the most surefire way for you to blow the interview. If you are late for an interview, the employer can only assume you will arrive late to work, turn in projects late, etc. On the flip side, do not show up more than fifteen minutes early. Showing up extremely early is also rude and puts additional pressure on the employer to accommodate you. If you arrive extremely early, go for a cup of coffee and come back about ten minutes prior to your scheduled time.

Sell yourself! Remember, the employer is interviewing you to see if you are a good fit. Everything you talk about during the interview should address this. Leave unrelated, personal information at the door. If the employer does not seem to be asking you many questions, offer information. You don't want to leave the interview feeling like you did not tell the employer enough about your qualifications.

# Never deny weaknesses. We all have them. One of
the most famous and most dreaded interview questions is, "What is
your greatest weakness?" Be honest here, but try to turn a negative into
a strength. For example, if your weakness is not delegating enough,
explain how you have been working on that problem and give examples
of how you have improved in recent months. Never say "I am a perfec-
tionist" or "I just work too hard" as your weakness. These are used all
the time, and the employer wants a well thought out, honest answer.

# Research the salary ranges for your field. The
employer may ask you what kind of salary you will expect. Be prepared
for this question by knowing what others make in the same market.

# Bring extra copies of your resume and reference lists to
the interview. Many times, there are people present in the interview
who have not yet seen your resume. Employers will most likely ask for
your reference list as well. Have it ready to give to them on the spot.
Make sure your references are current and expecting a phone call!
Three professional references is standard.

# Ask for the job! Make sure the employer knows how
much you want it. Be professional and assertive, not aggressive.

**INTERVIEW JOURNAL**

Find some quiet time with your journal to
consider the interview experience. This will
assist you incredibly with your job interviews.
Here's how:

Brainstorm and write down all possible
questions you can foresee coming at you in the
interview. Think about questions from each of
the following categories:

• Questions regarding anything and everything
you have listed on your resume

• Questions regarding your strengths and
weaknesses

• Situational questions, such as, "Tell me about
a time when you had a problem at work, and
how you solved it."

• Questions specific to the employer, relating to
your qualifications for the job

Now take some time to write out thoughtful
answers to these questions. Start early—this is
not something you want to do the night before
your interview! Write out answers to maybe two
or three questions per day in the weeks prior to
your interview date. It is amazing how this
helps to solidify your responses in your head.

# chapter 4
## MANIFESTING VISION

| | objective | outcome | readings | other elements |
|---|---|---|---|---|
| **unit 1** | Develop a clear sense of vision, direction, and purpose based on core values and creative passions. | Students will define the attributes of a personally meaningful and significant life, which reflects their innate gifts and talents.<br>Students will identify the roles they will play in the future and balance the energy they will give to each role.<br>Students will plan the steps for implementing their visions in the world. | Expressing Your Greatness<br>*A Return to Love*<br>Creating a Personal Mission Statement<br>*Making a Life*<br>Making Your Vision Concrete<br>*The Moral Imagination*<br>*Whole Life Review*<br>Setting Goals | Roles/Tributes Visualization<br>Mission Statement<br>Save the Last Word for Me<br>Life Choices<br>Balancing Roles |
| **unit 2** | Use imagination, creativity, and expressive media to envision the future. | Students will create and present to the class a final vision project and creator's statement that reflects their motivation and commitment to manifesting their vision in the world. | A Strong, Clear Vision<br>Samples of Creator's Statements | The Vision Project and Creator's Statement<br>Making a Project Proposal |

**MANIFESTING VISION**

*There is no greater joy than that of feeling oneself a
creator. The triumph of life is expressed by creation.*

HENRI BERGSON

**P**erhaps the most wonderful of all human gifts is our ability for creative imagination and expression. We all know that creative imaginations produce the great works of culture: the paintings of Van Gogh, the sonnets of Shakespeare, the buildings of Gehry. What some of us may not realize is that our gift of creativity is not limited to works of art, music, architecture, and literature. Creativity also allows us to discover our own personal greatness and to shape our unfolding life stories—our visions of what our lives will be like in the future and what important work we will want to accomplish. We all have a purpose to live out, based on our authentic gifts, skills, and abilities, which may lie buried and unacknowledged within us. Our ability for creative imagination can help us get in touch with our greatness and guide us to a wealth of possibilities for our lives.

Albert Einstein said, "Imagination is more important than knowledge." He knew that self-awareness, meaning, and purpose actually require acts of imagination. The problem is we often don't trust our imaginations. Our visions or fantasies of ourselves and our futures may seem silly or impractical or carry too much risk—we may not know what to make of them. Our imaginations, however, can lead us to the development of deeply fulfilling lives. The connection between our everyday lives and our imaginary worlds is where our visions for the future come alive. In fact, that is the most vital power of imagination: the intimate connection between our daily lives—our humdrum routines and schedules—and the exciting images and vision that glow beneath the surface.

Since we must envision our lives in order to create them, what is the vision for your life? Does it include artistic success? Financial freedom? Radiant health? Deeply fulfilling relationships? Travel? Inner peace? Service to others? A sense of connection to the world? Fulfilling spiritual needs? Only you have the power to create a life's vision that will inspire you, excite you, and lead you on a journey of wonder and discovery. The journey will be challenging, with important decisions to be made along the way. Which career to choose? To have a relationship or not? To say yes or no to that volunteer project? To get deeply involved in improving others' lives or concentrate on yourself? To follow your own dreams or your parents'? To give up or persevere? What commitments will you make? Which roads will you travel?

Creating and manifesting an empowering vision for our lives is an ongoing process. We must prioritize values, define what is important to us, and work on a specific plan for attaining and balancing the various roles we will play. We must also let our imaginations flow where they will and develop an attitude of success, even though obstacles will undoubtedly stand in our way. As we attempt to manifest our visions and travel on our own particular paths, we may encounter loneliness, vulnerability, and uncertainty. We will probably experience setbacks and limitations. But we will also discover deep satisfaction, wisdom, and a fuller understanding of our complex selves.

We are all shaped by our life choices and by our capacity for making and honoring our commitments. This chapter will help you make choices, define specific directions in your life to which you are willing to commit, and help you take the actions required to manifest your personal vision. You will find that during this process, deliberate and rational thinking is necessary, but also essential is listening to your heart's desires, acknowledging your dreams, and freeing your creative imagination. No one but you can determine your right path or whether your heart will be in it. So, let the vision quest begin.

# your vision

*Objective: Develop a clear sense of vision, direction, and purpose based on core values and creative passions.*

## unit one

**EXPRESSING YOUR GREATNESS**

**EXCERPT FROM A RETURN TO LOVE**

**CREATING A PERSONAL MISSION STATEMENT**

**EXCERPT FROM MAKING A LIFE**

**ROLES/TRIBUTES VISUALIZATION**

**MISSION STATEMENT**

**MAKING YOUR VISION CONCRETE**

**THE MORAL IMAGINATION**

**SAVE THE LAST WORD FOR ME**

**LIFE CHOICES**

**BALANCING ROLES**

**WHOLE LIFE REVIEW**

**SETTING GOALS**

## YOUR VISION

*Objective: Develop a clear sense of vision, direction, and purpose based on core values and creative passions.*

n order to have a strong and inspiring vision, we need to be in touch with the greatness of our passions, our purpose, and our values. It can sometimes be difficult to accept and express our greatness.

## EXPRESSING YOUR GREATNESS

In her book *A Return to Love,* Marianne Williamson charges us with living up to our potential. The speech can be the basis for inspiration for all of us.

excerpt from A RETURN TO Love

'Our deepest fear is not that we are inadequate.

Our deepest fear is that we are powerful beyond measure.

It is our light, not our darkness, that frightens us.'

We ask ourselves, Who am I to be brilliant, gorgeous, talented, fabulous?

Actually, who are you *not* to be?

You are a child of God.

Your playing small doesn't serve the world.

There's nothing enlightened about shrinking

so that other people won't feel insecure around you.

We are all meant to shine, as children do.

We were born to make manifest the glory of God that is within us.

It's not just in some of us; it's in everyone.

And as we let our own light shine,

by Marianne Williamson | we unconsciously give other people permission to do the same.

As we're liberated from our own fear,

our presence automatically liberates others.

?

*What line from the reading sticks out the most for you and why?*

*Why might it feel dangerous to express our greatness?*

*In what situations have you felt your greatness? What conditions supported this?*

*Within the learning community, you can participate in a group affirmation. Focusing on one person at a time, each community member states a quality they respect and value in the chosen person. They also briefly share where and how they saw that quality manifesting within the learning community.*

*After all the affirmations are completed, each person can discuss how it felt, why it might have been hard to take in the positive strokes, and what made it easier.*

## CREATING A PERSONAL MISSION STATEMENT

In a world where we have many decisions to make and myriad roles to play, creating a mission statement—a brief and focused statement of your unique purpose and meaning in life—can be empowering. A personal mission statement can focus our creative imaginations and crystallize the passion of our visions. It can also be used to initiate, evaluate, and refine our life's activities and will give us a sense of direction and excitement about our futures.

Some mission statements are significantly more empowering than others. Unless our mission statement creates a deep inner connection to our sense of purpose and meaning, it will not lead us to the profoundly satisfying lives that we all desire. In fact, many of us strive to achieve a sense of meaning and purpose by living our lives backward. We seek jobs, for example, that will allow us to make a great deal of money and that give us a high degree of status, and then later we try to find out what is really important in our lives.

●

excerpt from
MAKING A Life,
MAKING A
LIVING

by Mark Albion

*A study of business school graduates tracked the careers of 1,500 people from 1960 to 1980. From the beginning, the graduates were grouped into two categories. Category A consisted of people who said they wanted to make money first so that they could do what they really wanted to do later—after they had taken care of their financial concerns. Those in category B pursued their true interests first, sure that money eventually would follow. What percentage fell into each category?*

*Of the 1,500 graduates in the survey, the money-now category A's comprised 93 percent or 1,245 people. Category B risk takers made up 17 percent, or 255 graduates.*

*After twenty years there were 101 millionaires in the group. One came from Category A, 100 from category B.*

*The study's author, Srully Blotnick, concluded that "the overwhelming majority of people who have become wealthy have become so thanks to work they found profoundly absorbing.... Their 'luck' arose from the accidental dedication they had to an area they enjoyed."*

Creating a mission statement can help us define who we are and what we will find profoundly absorbing. As Epictetus said nearly two thousand years ago, "Know first who you are. Then dress accordingly." That, of course, takes reflection and action. It means throwing off the confining cloak of "should dos" and "have to dos" to find yourself and your inner greatness by doing the things you love to do and are good at doing. Though the mind knows the direction, the heart knows the path to creative and joyful purpose.

## ROLES/TRIBUTES VISUALIZATION

This visualization exercise, adapted from an exercise in the book *First Things First,* by Stephen Covey, Roger Merrill, and Rebecca Merrill, can help you create a mission statement that will help you define your right path. Take a few minutes to visualize your ninetieth birthday. Imagine a joyous celebration, where you are surrounded by dear friends, family, and colleagues who have come to celebrate and honor your life. Imagine the party in great detail: what will your surroundings be like, how will you be dressed, what time of year will it be, how many people will be there, and how will the room be decorated?

Imagine the people at this celebration paying tribute to you. Each individual is there to recall and honor a specific aspect of your life. Perhaps one of your teachers will be there or a former employer. Maybe you'll see a person to whom you lent a helping hand or a student you remember. There might be coworkers there, people you played sports with, and neighbors. They will be speaking of jobs and activities you performed particularly well, with passion and heartfelt care. Be sure to note the different roles you've played that are being honored, e. g., parent, performer, teacher, humanitarian. You may use the space on this page to record these roles and tributes.

What will these people say about you? What stories will they relate? How will they describe their relationships with you and the qualities about you that they remember the best? Will they talk about contributions that you made or improvements you instigated? Will they speak of joy you brought to other people or artistic talent that enlightened all who experienced your work? How did you make a difference in these people's lives?

How do you feel about these tributes and this glorious life of yours when you look back at it from your ninety-year-old perspective? Are you proud and satisfied by your life's work?

**Roles/Tributes**

As your reverie deepens, attempt to write down the various roles you played and why you are being honored for each one of them.

*Role #1*

*Tribute*

*Role #2*

*Tribute*

*Role #3*

*Tribute*

*Role #4*

*Tribute*

*Role #5*

*Tribute*

*Role #6*

*Tribute*

*Role #7*

*Tribute*

## MISSION STATEMENT

Now, based on these roles and tributes, you will want to create a mission statement that encapsulates your unique purpose and direction in life. Your mission statement can range from a few words to several pages. Some of you may even wish to express the statement in music, poetry, or art.

Here are several necessary components, excerpted from the book *First Things First,* to help you write your mission statement. An empowering mission statement:

- *represents the deepest and best within you. It comes out of a solid connection with your deep inner life.*

- *is the fulfillment of your own unique gifts. It's the expression of your unique capacity to contribute.*

- *is transcendent. It's based on principles of contribution and purpose higher than self.*

- *addresses and integrates all four fundamental human needs and capacities. It includes fulfillment in physical, social, mental, and spiritual dimensions.*

- *is based on principles that produce quality-of-life results. Both the ends and the means are based on true north principles.*

- *deals with both vision and principle-based values. It's not enough to have values without vision—you want to be good, but you also want to be good for something. On the other hand, vision without values can create a dictator. An empowering mission statement deals with both character and competence—what you want to be and what you want to do in your life.*

- *deals with all the significant roles in your life. It represents a lifetime balance of personal, family, work, community—whatever roles you feel are yours to fill.*

- *is written to inspire you—not to impress anyone else. It communicates to you and inspires you on the most essential level.*

*The Universe is transformation—our life is what our thoughts make it.*

MARCUS AURELIUS

It may also be helpful to read other people's mission statements, although some individuals feel it inhibits their own creative imagination. A few, from *First Things First*, are included here, and it's up to you whether or not you feel reading them would inspire your own statement.

*"Climb the mountain:*

*I will live each day with courage and a belief in myself and others. I will live by the values of integrity, freedom of choice, and a love of all God's people. I will strive to keep commitments not only to others but to myself as well. I will remember that to truly live, I must climb the mountain today, for tomorrow may be too late. I know that my mountain may seem no more than a hill to others and I will accept that. I will be renewed by my own personal victories and triumphs no matter how small. I will continue to make my own choices and to live with them as I have always done. I will not make excuses or blame others. I will, for as long as possible, keep my mind and body healthy and strong so that I am able to make the choice to climb the mountain. I will help others as best I can and I will thank those who help me along the way."*

*"To act in a manner that brings out the best in me and those important to me—especially when it might be most justifiable to act otherwise."*

*"I will maintain a positive attitude and a sense of humor in everything I do. I want to be known by my family as a caring and loving husband and father; by my business associates as a fair and honest person; and my friends as someone they can count on. To the people who work for me and with me, I pledge my respect and will strive every day to earn their respect. Controlling all my actions is a strong sense of integrity which I believe is the most important character trait."*

# Now write your mission statement.

Mentally go to a place of quiet, harmony, and balance so you can imagine your life's purpose and what matters to you most. Then create your statement from this rich, deep inner life, teeming with ideas and images and filled with a sense of wonder.

*Some men see things as they are and ask why. Others dream of things that never were and ask why not.*

GEORGE BERNARD SHAW

## MAKING YOUR VISION CONCRETE

# Now that you have a sense of a mission for your life, you can use it as a guide to making specific life choices. Before you begin the next

exercise, read "The Moral Imagination," by Stephen Asma. In it, Asma speaks of the importance of the imagination in creating a vision of how your life ought to be, in developing ethical values, and in recognizing that your daily choices and your long-term goals are part of a narrative that you create. To develop a balanced, moral, and healthy life, you must first imagine it in concrete detail. You must see it, feel it, and experience it in your mind and heart. As you read the article, think of a time when you used your imagination to solve a problem, create something, or express your vision of the future.

by Stephen T. Asma

Developing a vision of the good life, conceiving of "the way things ought to be" both in our communities and in ourselves, is largely the work of our imaginations. In order to make our individual lives and our societies more healthy, we must have the skill and creativity to imagine them enhanced in concrete detail. Through the imagination we can begin to remake ourselves in the image of our higher natures. And though we already engage in this activity all the time, we can certainly cultivate this imagination to a greater degree.

The "imagination" should not be confused with whimsical fantasy—we're not simply "making up" our moral goals as we go along. To recognize the role of imagination in our ethical lives is not to claim that our duties are figmentary, nor to claim that our moral goals are subjectively relative. It is simply recognizing that our day to day value choices and our long term goals are constantly responding to, revising, and rewriting themselves in light of the complexities and the flux of our experience. Doing the "right thing" in a given situation is not as simple as plugging some variables into a "morality equation" and merely deriving some inexorable solution. Having moral wisdom is not just grasping certain theoretical rules or propositions, "it is not even simply intellectual grasp of particular facts; it is perception. It is seeing a complex, concrete reality in a highly lucid and richly responsive way; it is taking in what is there, with imagination and feeling."(Nussbaum 1992, pg. 152)

When civil rights activists "dreamed" of a better society, they were not spinning ungrounded mental fantasies. They were imagining a way in which their current conditions, limitations and possibilities could be transformed into an attainable reality, and this imagination fired their convictions by holding out an almost palpable ideal before their mind's eye. Referring to the moral leadership of Justice Thurgood Marshall and Martin Luther King Jr., Edward Tivnan says, "they amaze and inspire us and help us reimagine the world we think we know so well, until we realize that something is so wrong with it that we have to create a new world." (1995, pg. 254) The imagination is the creative juncture between the raw material of our present and the perfected constructions of our future.

Our ethical lives are linked strongly to imagination in several ways. First, it is an imaginative act to envision ourselves behaving and living in a manner that we respect and esteem. When we make our personal career choices, relationship decisions, or we think about ourselves putting convictions into practice, we do so through an imaginative formulation of things that do not yet exist. We imagine the implications and consequences of our acts, and the detail and nuance we bring to those as yet unplayed dramas will determine whether or not we play out those dramas with open-eyes. Secondly, when we interact with other people and try to build community and tolerance out of the reality of disagreement, inequity and strife, we must think our way into the minds and lives of those who are different from ourselves. This difficult task of understanding and relating to people with radically different backgrounds and concerns, so crucial for effective democracy, is largely the work of empathic imagination. Well-to-do White suburbanites, for example, must try to imagine life as an underprivileged African American urbanite, and vice versa. Korean Americans must try to "walk a mile in the shoes" of Mexican American migrant workers, and vice versa. Catholics must imagine life as Muslims, and vice versa. Third, it is largely through imaginative works (literature, plays, films, etc.) that we develop moral possibility in our own lives (both potential moral successes and dangers). Art can give us much needed access to the inner lives and daily challenges of people who are quite different from ourselves. Amy Tan's novels, for example, gave non-Asian readers a powerful experience of the different values that inform Asian culture—helping non-Asians to better identify with and understand their own neighbors, co-workers, and friends. Zora Neal Hurston's novels, or the work of Alice Walker, shed similar light upon the African American experience for many people. Hip Hop music, for example, can bring very different people together, bridging cultures of ethnicity, geography, and economics. People frequently underestimate the role of art and imagery in the edification and inspiration of their own moral convictions. Yet the rich concrete detail of artwork (e.g., a literary novel) can clearly preserve the subtle intricacies of human relationships (their specific obligations and inclinations) in a way unparalleled by moral mandates or scholastic speculations. Through artwork, artists can convey moral visions and patrons can reflect upon them, reject or embrace them, take inspiration from them, and otherwise be enriched in a way that is more than merely aesthetic.

Many moral teachers have understood how effective the indirect methods of communication (i.e., analogy, metaphor, myth and parable) can be in imparting ethical ideas. And many artists have understood that their imaginative work can have moral power. Film makers have effectively challenged and animated our ethical values and writers have transmitted moral truths to us by showing us examples of dignity and depravity without preaching or proselytizing. The 19th century author George Eliot, for example, sought to increase our compassion for one another by portraying specific characters and story lines in her writings. She argued that morality was more than just local custom and more than just sophisticated theorizing from principles. "To lace ourselves up in formulas," she wrote, is to repress the "promptings and inspirations that spring from growing insight and sympathy." And those inspirations can be given and taken in good literature and other artforms.

Throughout our lives, we are constantly interacting with novels, films, plays and other artforms that raise questions and offer perspectives on human values. The moral imagination is already pervasive throughout our daily lives. If we are vigilant and reflective, we can bring this implicit process of self/social improvement into the realm of explicit action.

Nussbaum, Martha (1992) *Love's Knowledge: Essays on Philosophy and Literature;* Oxford University Press.

Tivnan, Edward (1995) *The Moral Imagination: Confronting the Ethical Issues of Our Day;* Simon & Schuster.

## SAVE THE LAST WORD FOR ME

A group exercise called *Save the Last Word for Me* (from the National School Reform Faculty) will help us clarify and deepen our thinking about "The Moral Imagination." This is a process designed to build on each other's thinking. It is not for entering into dialogue. Timing is important to the process; each round should last about seven minutes. The total time it will take is thirty minutes. The protocol is as follows:

Create a group of four participants. Choose a timekeeper who has a watch.

Each participant silently identifies what he/she considers to be the most significant idea addressed in the article.

When the group is ready, a volunteer identifies the point he/she found most significant in the article and reads it out loud to the group. The first person says nothing about why they chose that particular point.

The other three participants each have one minute to respond to that idea.

The first participant then has three minutes to state why they chose that point and to respond to his/her colleagues based on what he/she heard.

The same pattern is followed until all four members of the group have had a chance to have "the last word."

An inspiring guide

to finding meaning in one's life is the book *Living Myth: Personal Meaning as Way of Life* by D. Stephenson Bond. You may want to read this book to open the gates of your rich imagination and gain insights into the possibilities for your future.

## LIFE CHOICES

Now that we've had a chance to explore how to imagine our lives forward, it's time to be more specific about our life choices. In your journal, answer the following questions. They will help you decide what specifically you have to create in your life in order for you to say, "Yes, this is the empowering vision for my life and here is how I will live it out."

*What is the life that you want?*

*What will it look like when you have it?*

*What will it feel like when you have it?*

*What will you be doing behaviorally when you have it?*

*How will it reflect your gifts and talents?*

*What are the various roles you will be playing?*

*Who are you doing them with?*

*Where will you be doing them?*

*How will your life be different from the way it is now?*

*How will this life manifest your ethical and moral convictions?*

*What are the obstacles to obtaining this life?*

**BALANCING ROLES**

A sense of balance must be established for the various roles you will play in life, e.g., artist, student, job seeker, employee, spouse, involved citizen, parent volunteer. Without balance, you will be in a constant turmoil over your myriad commitments to each. Each commitment is important and each must be seen as an integral part of the totality of your lives. As Gandhi observed, "One man cannot do right in one department of life whilst he is occupied in doing wrong in another department. Life is one indivisible whole."

But how do you achieve this integration of the various parts of your life? As Stephen Covey, Roger Merrill, and Rebecca Merrill suggest in their book *First Things First,* make sure that each of your roles is connected to your vision and mission. This connection to vision and mission gives intensity, passion, and energy to your roles.

Go back to the "Roles/Tributes" exercise and analyze each of your roles in terms of what relationships it fosters and in what ways it holds you accountable to something higher than self. Whether you think of this something as God, future generations, society, or the world in general, it is important to feel a sense of connection to others and responsibility to a higher order.

•*Role*

•*How it connects to my vision/mission*

•*What relationships it fosters*

•*How it connects me to something higher*

# WHOLE LIFE REVIEW

Adapted from the book *Your Best Year Yet!* by Jinny Ditzler

Take a moment to reflect on the different roles you most identify with in your current life, e. g., graduating senior, artist, friend, son/daughter, seeker. Limit yourself to no more than eight roles.

Divide a circle into eight equal parts.

At the end of each spoke write the name of one of your life roles.

Imagine each spoke divided into ten equal segments. Let the rim of the circle be ten and the center zero. Decide how happy you are with your performance in each role. If you're completely satisfied with your performance, rate yourself a ten; if you're 50% satisfied, give yourself a five; if you're not doing anything at all or your performance is abysmal, you'll probably give yourself a zero.

Place a dot on each line at the point of your rating.

Join the dots to assess your overall level of performance and to see a picture of your current state of balance.

As you look at the results of your "Whole Life Review," ask yourself:

*What do these results mean to me?*

*What do I see in this overview of my life?*

*In which role am I performing the worst? The best?*

*Which roles am I giving enough time to? Not enough time?*

*What do I need or want to change first?*

Let your intuition and your imagination direct your thinking. Listen to the internal messages, both negative and positive. Do your best to make the process validating rather than invalidating. Increase your awareness of yourself as the observer—the chairman of the board. Use this opportunity to make a neutral assessment of how you are currently balancing the various roles in your life.

From these many roles, you will want to select a few to focus on for the next year of your life. In the next section, you'll be creating some specific goals to actualize during this important transitional period.

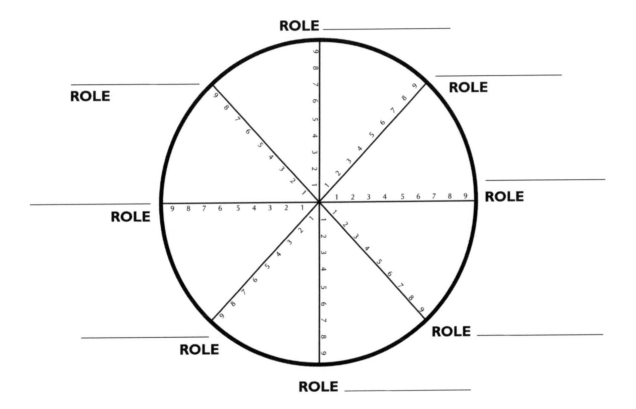

Diagram of Whole Life Review: Performance and Balance Check adapted from *Your Best Year Yet!* by Jinny Ditzler

## SETTING GOALS

Setting goals may be the most important step in manifesting your vision in the world. No matter how you define your vision, your chance of achieving it will be greater if you have clearly defined goals.

A goal is a specific and measurable result you want to achieve within a specific time frame. It directs you to a destination, a result, a career, an avocation, a relationship—something you haven't yet acquired or experienced in your life.

*If you have built castles in the air, your work need not be lost; that is where they should be. Now put the foundations under them.*

HENRY DAVID THOREAU

When you set goals and write them down, you've expressed your willingness to be responsible for living with integrity—doing what you know to do in order to be true to yourself and your vision. When your talents, your intelligence, and your awareness are directed at a specific target, this consolidation of energy brings results in a way a scattered approach fails to do.

Setting goals moves us from dreams with a remote possibility and reliance on blind luck to the results and relationships we're looking for. Living life with the attitude "Let's wait and see how it turns out" can be a waste of your potential and your power.

Powerful goals are specific. They are defined in words that give you a clear and concise mental image of what you want to achieve. You know from reading the goal exactly what you want. The more specific your goal, the more quickly you'll see what to do and be able to find resources to achieve it. Here are some examples of specific and nonspecific goals.

> Nonspecific goal: Live a stress-free life and increase my peace of mind.
>
> Specific goal: Meditate at least fifteen minutes each morning.
>
> Nonspecific goal: Improve my performance at work.
>
> Specific goal: Find out exactly what I need to do to get a promotion and a 4 percent pay raise, and do it.

*Nothing will work unless you do.*

MAYA ANGELOU

Powerful goals must be measurable. Quantify each goal so that you'll be in no doubt at the end of the semester whether you've won or lost the game or how close you came.

Powerful goals must be set in a time frame that includes specific three-month milestones. Limiting the time available to achieve your goal establishes focus. Goals without a deadline are meaningless.

Take a look at the following example:

> Goal: Write my first book and find an agent and publisher.
>
> Three-month milestones: Write chapter outline. Identify three potential agents.
>
> Six-month milestones: Write first three chapters. Attend a writer's conference.

Powerful goals start with strong, active verbs. They mark the start of your goal, which will be a simple and complete sentence. For example: Give, Earn, Practice, Write, Spend time, Complete, Arrange, Plan, Get, Choose, Invest, Achieve, Learn, Work, Ensure, Make, Meet.

When writing your goals, first distinguish between result goals and process goals:

> Result Goals: Achieve sales target of $100,000.
>
> Process Goal: Make twenty new sales calls each week.
>
> Result Goal: Improve networking and communications.
>
> Process Goal: Attend an "industry" meeting or meet with a new contact in my target career field twice a month.

Next, review the various roles you've identified on the whole life review. Choose one or two roles as your major focus during this important transition period. Where are you going to put the greatest emphasis? What would be your most important result goal at the end of the year in relation to this role or roles?

*ROLE*

*RESULT GOAL:*

*PROCESS GOALS:*
*(include steps, measurements, and deadlines)*

*Adapted from* Your Best Year Yet! *by Jinny Ditzler*

# One final check.

Before finalizing your goals for the year, go through the list, thinking carefully about each and asking yourself questions such as the following:

*Will I make this happen?*

*Am I merely hoping this will be achieved simply because it's on the list?*

*Am I going to do this?*

*Is this goal specific and measurable?*

*Does it start with a verb?*

*Is this a result or process goal? Are the steps and deadlines clear?*

*Do these goals match my values?*

*Do I want this goal badly enough to do what it takes?*

*Am I willing to be responsible for this goal?.*

# Now let's make it happen.
Close your eyes for a minute and think about how you're going to feel when you accomplish each result goal. What will you do to celebrate? Think about how you will reward yourself for each result goal and make a note in the margin by that goal.

Write your goals in your journal and/or on an index card. Keep them visible, think about them, and refer to them frequently.

Next to each goal, write the names of people who can serve as coaches and helpers. Then create an action plan with dates and activities to achieve your goals.

Choose at least one process goal to achieve by next week. Choose something that you are sure you can accomplish. Be prepared to report back to your classmates.

# expressing
## your vision

**A STRONG, CLEAR VISION**

**THE VISION PROJECT AND CREATOR'S STATEMENT**

**MAKING A PROJECT PROPOSAL**

**SAMPLES OF CREATOR'S STATEMENT**

## unit two

*Objective: Use imagination, creativity, and expressive media to envision the future.*

## EXPRESSING YOUR VISION

*Objective: Use imagination, creativity, and expressive media to envision the future.*

*Vision is the art of seeing things invisible.*

JONATHAN SWIFT

**N**ow that we've explored our vision through working on a mission statement, setting goals, and setting up an action plan for achieving those goals, we may find a compelling urge to express that vision in a creative manner. We can look to others who have led visionary lives for inspiration. One such person is Maya Lin.

## A STRONG, CLEAR VISION

The video *Maya Lin: A Strong Clear Vision* won the 1995 Academy Award for best feature documentary. It documents a decade of architect/artist Maya Lin's creations. Maya Lin is the designer of the Vietnam Veterans Memorial and the civil rights memorial among others. She is the daughter of Chinese immigrants. This video relates well to your vision project partly because Maya Lin was also completing a class project as a twenty-one-year-old student at Yale when she created the design for the Vietnam Memorial. Maya Lin speaks eloquently about her passion for her work and her belief in the ability of art to deal with the issues of our times in a healing and restorative manner.

*What stood out most about this video?*

*What is Maya Lin's strong, clear vision?*

*What obstacles did Maya have to face, and how did she overcome them?*

*What is your strong, clear vision?*

*In what ways can you use the final project experience in this class to express your vision?*

# THE VISION PROJECT
# AND CREATOR'S STATEMENT

As you develop your own strong, clear vision, you may choose to express that vision in a creative project. Our most fulfilling work is when the joy of creative self-expression is matched with the sense of satisfaction that comes from doing something meaningful. Each of us can have a positive impact with what we have to offer.

The Vision Project will stand as a representative work of who you are and where your passion/purpose/values, vocation, and sense of service intersect. Choose a medium with which you have a sense of voice, through which you are expressive and can enthusiastically engage, and in which you can achieve the best possible quality of presentation. Consider projects/ideas that you may have always had to put on hold because of other commitments.

Possible ideas include business plans, ad campaigns, performance pieces, visual works, Web pages, videos, photographs, books, articles, fashions, poetry, fiction, and speeches.

The creator's statement will be a written expression of your vision project. In the creator's statement you will discuss the following items:

## MEANING

*Why were you drawn to this project?*

*Why is it important to you?*

*What did you learn/discover while doing the vision project?*

## SIGNIFICANCE

*Who is the audience you wish to reach?*

*Who is the community being served, celebrated, or illuminated?*

*What would be the ideal effect of this work upon the audience (the meaning of the work)?*

## EXECUTION

*What was your process in creating the project?*

*How was the medium you chose appropriate to the intended purpose of the project?*

*How were details (color, texture, fonts, symbols, size) used to enhance the meaning of the project?*

Both the vision project and the creator's statement will be presented and evaluated in class. You will want to present yourself and your project professionally.

*A bit of advice given to a young Native American at the time of his initiation: "As you go the way of life, you will see a great chasm.*

*Jump.*

*It is not as wide as you think."*

JOSEPH CAMPBELL

## MAKING A PROJECT PROPOSAL

As you begin working on your vision project, it is important to be inspired and ready to express your greatness and your vision. Remember what Marianne Williamson said in her book *Return to Love*: "Our deepest fear is not that we are inadequate. Our deepest fear is that we are powerful beyond measure…. Your playing small doesn't serve the world." In this project and other endeavors in your life, aspire to be and express your greatness.

There will be many occasions in your life when you will need to pitch an idea to someone for funding or support of some kind. The following activity will provide you with experience in speaking inspirationally of your own plans and ideas.

Working in groups of three, you may complete the following experience.

You will present your ideas for your vision project as follows:

- Describe the medium you have chosen and why (drawing, writing, video, performance, marketing plan).
- Describe why you are drawn to the project (personal meaning).
- Describe who you are hoping to reach and how (inspiring youth, celebrating a culture, giving the gift of laughter to those in pain, educating the well about an illness).
- Describe your plans for completion of the project (steps, dates).

The other members of the group will then respond as follows:

- Describe what moved you most about the intended project.
- Question matters that need clarification for you.
- Provide creative ideas you may have thought of as you heard about the project as suggestions.

You will then respond to the information shared by your peers as follows:

- Clarify anything as needed.
- Respond to creative suggestions as to whether or not they sparked ideas for you.
- Summarize whether or not you feel your classmates fully understood the scope and intent of your project.

While you leave the room for a moment, your peers will confer about the following:

- Are the voice, values, and vision of the creator evident in the project?
- Is the project innovative and inspiring?
- Is the project relevant, socially significant, fulfilling a need?
- Is the target audience apparent?
- Is it realistic to excellently execute the project by the deadline?

Your peers will present their "evaluation" of your project to you using constructive language, positive feedback, and suggestions for improvement.

## SAMPLES OF CREATOR'S STATEMENTS

Read the following creator's statements and project descriptions for inspiration in creating your own project. You may also view the *Senior Seminar* videos for inspiration.

Boy Crazy is a portfolio of photographs illustrating the emotional stress women go through after a relationship breakup. Through the medium of blue printing, I am able to release the damaging memories that haunt women while they lie on their beds at night. I created these images to bring to light the misery of weeping over a past relationship, the loneliness of not having a father for your newborn son, the depression of being alone, and the devastation of breaking up. I shot these pictures as a mirror to the brokenhearted, presenting a chain of reflections of naive and married women. My intent is to cultivate a therapeutic awakening. This awakening will bring forth change in the lives of women who have confronted similar situations.

My audience will be women from the ages of fifteen to twenty-five. I would like to present these images in high schools and colleges around the nation. I created these photographs with the Cyanotype process on brown paper. Blue is known to be the color of sadness, and the brown paper will give a paper bag effect that will bring forth an aura of disposable baggage.

Asia Hamilton
*Boy Crazy*
2002

Although this portfolio is geared toward the above demographic, it will spark the attention of all people. It will move the hearts of people as they can relate to the subject. There are many women crying right now feeling all alone, many women who think there is no hope, many women who feel that nobody can relate to their distress. I hope to show them that there is someone who can share in their pain. This portfolio will hold a visual monologue of women who have gone Boy Crazy!

There comes a time in one's life when a revelation rears its head and you begin to change. For some, this change is a bad one, but for most the revelation is a life-altering event which only turns out for the best. I just happen to be one of the lucky ones.

I seem to be able to pinpoint certain moments where I see beauty when others don't. For example, in drawing class we sketched drapery. Most classmates complained, griped, and moaned about it, but shine a light on the folds of the fabric, watch the shadows and how they fall, and there is beauty.

Aaron Ingle
*Vision Project*
2002

A movie came out a couple of years ago, *American Beauty*. There was a scene where two characters watched video of a plastic bag floating in the air. One character said, "Sometimes there is so much beauty in the world that I just can't take it." That scene really struck a chord with me. I felt what he was saying.

I found an old abandoned couch and I took pictures of it. As I developed these photos, I was fascinated as somebody's garbage took on meaning. They had emotion; the shapes, lines, and shadows in the images were all so beautiful. But from waste? From garbage? Is that possible? I assure you it is. I found another couch, and it happened again.

My Vision Project is a book I made. And this book is a perfect representation of my whole philosophy. I wanted to get my theme across (beauty is within), so I decided to make the cover not look like the stereotypical book cover. I tried to make it look rough, junky, ugly even. The pages that contain the photographs are made from cardboard I cut from various boxes; the edges are jagged and the backsides are exposed. All these layers help the viewer to learn to look closer at things. I think each experience will be unique to the individual viewer, which is really the whole purpose anyway.

I think people today are told to think what is and what isn't beautiful. I don't want to be a part of that, and I hope that each viewer will get something unique out of it for themselves.

# I decided to do a painting that would reflect a view of the Japanese people. I cannot represent the entire people, but I thought that some people see things the way I do.

Naotsugu Kono
*Patriotism*
2002

For this class, I had a hard time choosing a topic. I was about to do a painting about the September 11 attack, but since it was the front cover topic, I chose not to. However, this changed when I received a call from my friend, telling me that there was something she wanted to show me. It was a mural that said, America will not forget September 11, 2002, and December 7, 1941. I immediately thought I had to make a painting about the feeling this provoked within me. I felt uncomfortable about these two dates being considered for the same category, and the words "America" and "Forget." When I went back home to Tokyo, I discussed this with lots of people, including through the Internet, and I finally decided to paint.

The painting I did has a dark American national flag as a background, and the front says, "9-11 = 12-7? What about 8-6?" The numbers are not equations; they are dates. I made them look like equations to show that the two dates are not the same. $9-11 = -2$ and $12-7 = 5$, therefore they are not equal. August 6 is the day when the atomic bomb was dropped on Hiroshima. I think that September 11 and Pearl Harbor were totally different events. The only thing that is the same is that they were both attacks on America, and that they were surprise attacks. The part that I liked least about the mural was the part that said, "will not forget." To me, that sounds like those two events are the only important events in American history. What about the bombing of Hiroshima?

People can be blinded by the emotional power of patriotism. What is patriotism? Is the nationality so important? We are all the same human beings. It is good that people love this country, and I am one of them, that is why I am here. However, I am afraid that the patriotism in America is only creating a notion that America is just, and always number 1, which I doubt sometimes.

Television major Mario Monrroy has an acquaintance whose son is autistic. Mario was learning about the West Suburban Special Recreation Association (WSSRA), and he asked what a group of art/media students could possibly do to make a difference for the organization. WSSRA responded that they could use a video to promote their services and volunteer opportunities.

Mario and his classmate, television major Linnea Campbell, produced, shot, and edited the video. Classmate Emily Pesce, an animation major, made an original video sleeve using photographs and graphics from the video. Tom Kasalo, a radio/sound major, provided his professional voice to engineer the narration and to make the project complete.

It was absolutely amazing to see the collective plan come to life, especially since most of this project's collaborators completed school projects individually. The team reports, "Our 'Creative Collaboration' section of Senior Seminar certainly lived up to its name. We all gained invaluable experience working in one another's disciplines." They agree that one or two of them making this video would not have resulted in as great a production as the final product of all of their work together.

Says the team: "This real-world knowledge of team work will undoubtedly help us all when we graduate, but most important to us, our project will actually help a very special group of people."

Mario Monrroy
Linnea Campbell
Emily Pesce
Tom Kasalo
*West Suburban Special Recreation Association Promotional Video*
2002

I had two main interests in taking portraits of the workers at Sloan Valve. First, I wanted to introduce to the art community a wise, but often dismissed community. Second, I wanted to revisit my previous employers and friends to see how they are faring, and to show them what I'm doing with my life now.

My familiarity with Sloan began when I joined my father as an employee in 1998. Interestingly, I decided to take the factory job so I could afford to pursue my interests in photography. Spending ten-hour shifts with working class people, different from my own family only in ethnicity, really opened my eyes to a wisdom gained from life experiences—hard life experiences. The friends I made at Sloan have had an invaluable impact on the way I see my world, and on the way I see other people.

Daniel Ramos
*Vision Project*
2002

One of the difficulties of working in the factory was trying to nurture a dream while being surrounded by disillusioned people. It is hard to keep hope alive in a place where harsh realities make meeting simple needs nearly impossible. My friends and coworkers were supportive of me, but not of my ambitions. My own father was among those who deemed me crazy for leaving a steady job to pursue art.

Going back to the factory, I am reminded of how lucky I am to have escaped such a mundane existence. I want my friends there to see what I'm doing now as a sign of hope for themselves and their children. And I want them to see in the pictures I take that they are valuable human beings.

tonika todorova
*Lost*
2002

# My Vision Project is called "Lost." It was written at a time

when what mattered to me had become lost, and although I am still searching, I have come to terms with that loss. I am sharing this with others because it is so personal to me. The only way I can find comfort is to know that if people are honest with their emotions, others will follow, resulting in everyone becoming stronger. Those who see my presentation need only get one thing out of it—an understanding that we are all human. We all grieve and laugh for the same reasons.

Theatre is my passion. My solo performance is a vulnerable venue, and it is very straightforward. It's just the human being and all its imperfections and hopes. The mutation of my performance is a constant process, and in ten years, what I have to say could be from a completely different point of view. If I had ten years, I am sure the incubation period would make the performance less self-indulgent, however every piece of art is a representation of the artist, so self-indulgence is probably an asset. I have learned that the human nature will always heal, grow, and have the desire to comprehend the reason for existence. As paradoxical as it may sound, maybe the reason we are here is to search for that reason eternally, without losing hope, or love and appreciation for ourselves and each other.

As we embark on a new millennium, and technology becomes the way of the future, we must not forget that we are human. I see myself as a reminder for those who have forgotten, or as a post-it of "Carpe Diem," or as a collector of human emotions. We are not alone. Maybe, just maybe, if we learn about ourselves through others, we can become better.

# TO BE THAT
# LIGHT
## THAT I HAVE SEEN

by Bill Hayashi
Director, Senior Seminar

There once was a girl named Allie, who more than anything else loved the Light.

Whenever she would look into the air, she would watch for the motes of dust sparkling in the beams of sunlight. When she was near water, she became entranced by the patterns of light reflecting on the water's surface, like shining diamonds. She would stare for hours at the luminous flames of a fire. When she would close her eyes, she would watch for the moving waves of red and sometimes purple/blue dots that moved mysteriously within the darkness in front of her. Most of all, she loved the light she saw shining in the eyes of children when they were happy and of grown-ups when they felt love. One day, she discovered she could capture this Light in music she made up on the piano. She called this music her "golden, shining songs." Allie was happiest of all when she could play these songs for people, who could feel the Light in the sounds cascading from inside her, which came directly from her own heart.

Once, when she was about seven, she came running into the house holding a handful of beautiful brown mud sparkling with flecks of bright sunlight. She ran to show her mother her treasure. Her mother, however, scolded her for bringing such filth into the house. She would dirty up the clean living-room floor. Her mom told her to take that mess outside and to use more common sense in the future. After that, Allie no longer looked for the Light in the elements of nature. And her world became less bright.

When she was seventeen, Allie fell in love with a boy with golden brown skin and the brightest pair of eyes she had ever seen. She decided to bring him home to meet her parents. After he left, her mother and father told her that he was a very nice boy but that since he had dark skin and she had light skin, they would have a lot of trouble being together in this world and that any child born to them would be open to much pain. They told her there was a big difference between choosing friends and partners, and that it would be best for everybody concerned if she dated only people of her own kind. After that, Allie no longer looked for the Light in people's skin and eyes. And her world became even less bright.

When she was twenty-one, Allie decided to give a recital of all her favorite "golden, shining songs." She invited all her friends and relatives, and even people who did not know Allie but who had heard of her music came to listen, too. The next day, there was a review in the town's paper by the local art critic. He said that Allie's music had a lot of passion, for a beginner, but that it lacked structure and complexity and that she needed to study theory and counterpoint and strengthen her technique as well. After that, Allie no longer listened for the Light in her music; indeed, she stopped playing for others altogether. And all the shining in her world went out.

When it came time for Allie to choose a career, she decided to go into human resources, since, as her parents told her, she was very good with people. She decided to move into the city where she would have more opportunities and where she could make the right contacts. Allie really was good with people and sensitive to what they wanted. She knew how to please them. Over time, she became quite, quite successful. She lived in an elegant high-rise apartment and had many interesting friends. And yet, Allie was not happy. She felt that something was missing in her life. She kept asking herself, "Is this all there is, all that's meant to be?" The only time Allie actually felt truly happy was when she would sit at the piano in her elegant apartment and play some of the golden, shining songs from her childhood. Then she would remember her love for the Light and for the simple joys of nature and for people who moved her. And she remembered how much she loved playing music that poured spontaneously from inside her heart.

One evening, after attending a very high-powered conference on human resources in a big downtown hotel, Allie noticed a beautiful grand piano sitting in the lobby. Feeling a bit bored and out-of-sorts, Allie sat down at the piano and began playing some of her golden, shining songs. As she lost herself in her music, an older, kindly man sat down on a sofa close by and began to listen to her. He closed his eyes, and as Allie continued to play, he relived memories of light and joy and love from his own youth. When she finished, he went up to her and thanked her for her beautiful music and for the impact it had had on him. He asked her whether she would be performing again the next night, because, if so, he wanted to come and hear her again. When she explained that she played only occasionally now and always just for herself, he asked her why. She said she had chosen human resources as her profession, which took up most of her time, and that though it didn't fully satisfy her, it provided a good income. The man told her, if she wanted to be truly happy, then she needed to play her own music. He told her we are happy only when we live from our own Light, and that we can do that only if and when we live and play our heart songs. "Who will sing your heart song if you don't?" he asked her.

This question, "Who will sing your heart song if you don't?" penetrated Allie's core. She suddenly remembered why she had written these songs, what had inspired them: the shining in earth, water, fire, and air; the light in people's skin and in their eyes; the luminous flow of golden music pouring forth directly from her own heart. And Allie wept as she remembered what had brought her so much bliss as a child. She thanked the man for recognizing and honoring what had once been her passion. She thanked him for reminding her of what she had once seen and been. He smiled at her and said, "Yes, to be truly happy, to be fully ourselves, we must be the Light that we have seen."

Allie made a career shift in midlife. She began to perform her music around the city.

Doors mysteriously opened and unseen hands appeared out of nowhere to provide support. She began to record and to appear on radio and television. She began receiving mail from people who longed for the Light that was in her music and who felt inspired and uplifted by it. She began doing workshops to help people find that Light within themselves and discover ways to best express their own unique music. She entitled her workshops, "Who will sing your heart song if you don't?" Allie became very successful and much beloved. She now serves thousands of people, helping them discover their passions, live their dreams. She now urges all of us to live out of our own inner shining, to radiate forth the Light that we have seen. And she always begins her workshops by asking, "Where and when have you seen that Light?"

*Move forward in the direction of your dreams.*

BILL HAYASHI

To be that light that I have seen.
COLUMBIA COLLEGE MOTTO

# BIBLIOGRAPHY

Ad Council and Music Television. "Engaging the Next Generation: How Nonprofits Can Reach Young Adults." On-line. Available at http://www.adcouncil.org/research/engaging_next_gen.

Albion, Mark. *Making a Life, Making a Living: Reclaiming Your Purpose and Passion in Business and in Life.* New York: Warner Books, 2000, 17.

Castaneda, Carlos. *The Teachings of Don Juan: A Yaqui Way of Knowledge.* New York: Pocket Books, 1975, 106-7.

Covey, Stephen R., A. Roger Merrill, and Rebecca R. Merrill. *First Things First: To Live, to Love, to Learn, to Leave a Legacy.* New York: Simon & Schuster, 1994, 107-9, 113, 318, 320, 321.

Csikszentmihalyi, Mihaly. *Flow: The Psychology of Optimal Experience.* New York: Harper Perennial, 1991, 39-40.

Dass, Ram and Mirabai Bush. *Compassion in Action: Setting Out on the Path of Service.* New York: Bell Tower, 1992. 172-79.

Didion, Joan. *Slouching Towards Bethlehem.* New York: The Noonday Press, 1990, 134-35, 138-39.

Ditzler, Jinny S. *Your Best Year Yet! Ten Questions for Making the Next Twelve Months Your Most Successful Ever.* New York: Warner Books, 1994, 147-50, 153-55, 206-7.

Dunn, Stephen. "The Last Hours." In *Different Hours.* New York: W. W. Norton, 2000, 55-56.

Jones, Michael. "Listening for the Deeper Music in Our Life and Work." *Spirit at Work Newsletter.* Edited by Judi Neal, May 1998. On-line. Available at http://www. pianoscapes.com/writingframe.html.

King, Stephen. "What You Pass On." *Family Circle Magazine,* November 2001, 156.

Lore, Nicholas. *The Pathfinder: How to Choose or Change Your Career for a Lifetime of Satisfaction and Success.* New York: Simon & Schuster, 1998, 116-17.

Myers, Isabel Briggs, et al. *MBTI Manual: A Guide to the Development and Use of the Myers-Briggs Type Indicator Third Edition.* Palo Alto, Calif.: Consulting Psychologists Press, 1998, 286-88.

Neruda, Pablo. "Poetry." In *Pablo Neruda: Selected Poems: A Bilingual Edition.* Edited by Nathaniel Tarn, translated by Anthony Kerrigan, W. S. Merwin, Alastair Reid, and Nathaniel Tarn. New York: Houghton Mifflin, 1990, 457, 459.

Oliver, Mary. "The Journey." In *New and Selected Poems.* Boston: Beacon Press, 1992, 114-15.

Putnam, Robert D. *Bowling Alone: The Collapse and Revival of American Community.* New York: Simon & Schuster, 2001, 18-20, 27, 44, 446, 493.

Remen, Rachel Naomi. "In the Service of Life." Institute of Noetic Sciences Fourth Annual Conference, "Open Heart, Open Mind," San Diego, Calif., July 1995.

Williams, Jean. "New Ways to Network: It's Not Who You Know, But Who Knows You." *Chicago Tribune,* 9 April 2000, Chicagoland final edition, 3.

Williamson, Marianne. *A Return to Love: Reflections on the Principles of A Course in Miracles.* New York: Harper Perennial, 1992, 190-91.

## CREDITS

Page 38
"Listening for the Deeper Music in Our Life and Work", by Michael Jones
Michael Jones is a pianist, composer, author and educator. His web site is www.pianoscapes.com. Used with permission of the author.

Page 46
"The Last Hours" from *Different Hours* by Stephen Dunn. Copyright © 2000 by Stephen Dunn. Used by permission of W. W. Norton & Company, Inc.

Page 47
"The Journey" from *Dream Work* by Mary Oliver. Copyright © 1986 by Mary Oliver. Used by permission of Grove/Atlantic, Inc.

Page 48
"Poetry" from *Selected Poems* by Pablo Neruda, translated by Alastair Reid, edited by Nathanial Tarn and published by Jonathan Cape. Used by permission of The Random House Group Limited.

Page 59
"What You Pass On" by Stephen King
Reprinted with permission. © Stephen King. All rights reserved.

Page 64
Reprinted with the permission of Simon & Schuster from *Bowling Alone: The Collapse and Revival of American Community* by Robert D. Putnam. Copyright © 2000 by Robert D. Putnam.

Page 70
From "Engaging the Next Generation: How Nonprofits Can Reach Young Adults" by The Advertising Council. Copyright © by The Advertising Council. Reprinted by permission.

Page 72
"In the Service of Life" by Rachel Naomi Remen
This article first appeared in the IONS Review and is reprinted by permission of the author and the Institute of Noetic Sciences (website: www.noetic.org). Copyright © 2002 by IONS, all rights reserved.

Page 75
From *Compassion in Action* by Ram Dass and Mirabai Bush, copyright © 1992 by Ram Dass and Mirabai Bush. Used by permission of Bell Tower, a division of Random House, Inc.

Page 110
"New Ways to Network: It's Not Who You Know, But Who Knows You" by Jean A. Williams
From Chicago Tribune, 4/9/2000 by Jean A. Williams. Copyright © 2000 by Jean Williams. Reprinted by permission of the author.